MAY 1 9 2015

PRAGUE

|CONDENSED|

paul smitz

LONELY PLANET PUBLICATIONS
Melbourne • Oakland • London • Paris

contents

Prague Condensed
1st edition – May 2002

Published by
Lonely Planet Publications Pty Ltd
ABN 36 005 607 983
90 Maribyrnong St, Footscray, Vic 3011, Australia
www.lonelyplanet.com or AOL keyword: lp

Lonely Planet offices
Australia Locked Bag 1, Footscray, Vic 3011
☎ 03 8379 8000   fax 613 8379 8111
e talk2us@lonelyplanet.com.au
USA   150 Linden St, Oakland, CA 94607
☎ 510 893 8555 Toll Free: 800 275 8555
fax 510 893 8572
e info@lonelyplanet.com
UK   10a Spring Place, London NW5 3BH
☎ 020 7428 4800 fax 020 7428 4828
e go@lonelyplanet.co.uk
France   1 rue du Dahomey, 75011 Paris
☎ 01 55 25 33 00 fax 01 55 25 33 01
e bip@lonelyplanet.fr
www.lonelyplanet.fr

Design Jacqui Saunders Maps Ray Thomson & Gus
Balbontin Editing Susie Ashworth & Darren O'Connell
Cover Jenny J Jones Publishing Manager Diana Saad
Thanks to David Burnett, Ryan Evans, Liz Filleul,
Quentin Frayne, Gabrielle Green, Mark Griffiths, James
Hardy, Annie Horner, Birgit Jordan, Rowan McKinnon,
Charles Rawlings-Way & Celia Wood

Photographs
Many of the images in this guide are available for
licensing from Lonely Planet Images:
www.lonelyplanetimages.com

Front cover photographs
Top A row of colourful house facades on the southern
side of the Old Town Square (Richard Nebeský)
Bottom Standing on the underground platform of
Můstek metro station in Nové Město (Richard Nebeský)

ISBN 1 74059 349 9

how to use this book

SYMBOLS

- ⊠ address
- ☎ telephone number
- Ⓜ nearest metro station
- 🚊 nearest train station
- 🚊 nearest tram route
- 🚗 auto route, parking details
- ◷ opening hours
- ⓘ tourist information
- ⑤ cost, entry charge
- **e** email/website address
- ♿ wheelchair access
- ⅄ child-friendly
- ✕ on-site or nearby eatery
- **V** good vegetarian selection

AUTHOR AUTHOR !

Paul Smitz

Paul is a one-time Prague ignoramus who now feels warmly enamoured of the Czech city and its amusing, bemusing and joy-inducing environs and inhabitants (translation: he really likes the place).

Regarding all of the stuff in the surrounding pages, he'd like to thank Katie for *výstup a nástup* the Prague express, Richard, Lenka, Markéta, Olda, Míra, Margarite, Oldřiška and Åse. Special thanks to his liver, and to Lusha for the chair.

COLOUR-CODING

Each chapter has a different colour code which is reflected on the maps for quick reference (eg all Highlights are bright yellow on the maps).

MAPS

The fold-out maps inside front and back covers are numbered from 1 to 7. All sights and venues in the text have map references which indicate where to find them on the maps; eg (3, A1) means Map 3, grid reference A1. Although each item is not pinpointed on the maps, the street address is always indicated.

PRICES

Price gradings (eg, 10/5Kč) usually indicate adult/concession entry charges to a venue. Concession prices can include senior, student, member or coupon discounts.

READER FEEDBACK

Things change – prices go up, schedules change, good places go bad and bad places improve or go bankrupt. So, if you find things better or worse, recently opened or long since closed, please tell us and help make the next edition even more accurate. Send all correspondence to the Lonely Planet office closest to you (listed on p. 2) or visit www.lonelyplanet.com/feedback/.

facts about prague

Historically rich Prague has a vivacious personality which has gone on a decade-long shopping spree and bought itself a new, hip wardrobe. Its boulevards and laneways have outstanding combinations of the classically old and the head-spinningly modern. Grandly preserved buildings on stone-floored streets host stylish bars and restaurants, while sculpture-encrusted theatres and Romanesque cellars echo with the sounds of orchestras and musos jazzing or rocking themselves into a sweat.

Not that this is any secret. Visitors have been coming to Prague for years to absorb the magnificent architectural legacies of castles and churches, and the commercial whirlwind of creative arts. Prague's rampant popularity is obvious to anyone who's been confronted with a tourist pack sweeping towards them down one of the city's narrow streets like a tsunami, leaving them clinging to an old building in its wake. But

even the crowds can sometimes add something special, like when you're sitting in a small *náměstí* and suddenly it fills with a tide of people who just as quickly depart, leaving you to savour their transience and appreciate the solitude even more.

The locals can sometimes be famously indifferent, but often this is just a tourist-weary facade or an indigenous bluntness. Don't be fooled into thinking that a gruff noise is the start and end of communication – shrug your assumptions to the floor, try a few words of broken Czech, and see what happens. Not bad as a mantra for your stay in Prague, really.

A warren of narrow streets and laneways wind through historic Malá Strana.

HISTORY
In the Beginning
People have been bunking down in the general area around Prague since 600,000BC, and farming communities settled here from 4000BC. The region was then occupied by Germanic and Celtic tribes, and in the 6th century, two Slav tribes, the Czechs and the Zličani, settled on either side of the Vltava.

The Czech Přemysl dynasty established Prague Castle in the 870s. Christianity was adopted during the rule of 'Good King' Wenceslas from 925-35, and in 950 Bohemia was engulfed by the Holy Roman Empire. Under Charles IV's rule (1346-78), Prague prospered and acquired landmarks like Charles Bridge and St Vitus Cathedral.

Hussites & Hapsburgs
Jan Hus led his Christian-reform movement (Hussitism) in the late 14th and early 15th centuries. He was burned at the stake in 1415, provoking a rebellion that eventually put the Hussites in charge; their king from 1452-71 was George of Poděbrady. The Czech nobility arranged for the Austrian Catholic Hapsburgs to rule in 1526, and Prague became the Hapsburg seat. But an uprising in 1618 resulted in the Thirty Years' War, the deaths of a quarter of the region's population, and ultimately the loss of Czech independence for two-and-a-half centuries.

Czech National Revival
Literature, journalism, architecture and drama flourished in Prague during the 19th-century Czech National Revival. One attempt to reclaim Czech identity was historian František Palacký's seminal *Dějiny národu českého* (History of the Czech Nation). In 1861, Czechs finally wrested control of Prague in council elections, but the country remained under Austrian rule.

A Word of Hurt
Czechs are responsible for the introduction of a rather unpleasant word to the English language. The word is 'defenestration', which means 'the act of throwing a thing or especially a person out of a window'. It was coined in 1419 when Hussites, still angry about the execution of their figurehead four years earlier, threw several Catholic councillors out of an upper window of Prague's New Town Hall. The incident was reprised with devastating consequences in 1618 (Thirty Years' War anyone?) when a couple of Hapsburg councillors left Prague Castle against their will, and it wasn't by the front door.

Independence & War
An unwillingness to support Austrian or Hungarian WWI causes led to international pleas from Czechs and Slovaks for independence, and on 28 October 1918, Czechoslovakia was born. Its capital was Prague, which immediately expanded by swallowing surrounding settlements.

By 1939 German forces had occupied Bohemia and Moravia. By the time WWII concluded, the Nazis had devastated nearly all of Prague's 120,000-strong Jewish population. One of the newly reinstated government's first acts was to expel Sudeten Germans, and thousands perished in forced marches to Bavaria and Austria.

Communism

The Communist Party won over one-third of the Czechoslovakian popular vote in the 1946 elections and formed a coalition government with other socialist parties. But after intense bickering with local democrats, the communists seized control with the Soviet Union's

Richard Nebeský

Today, the National Theatre still bears the scars of the 1968 Soviet invasion.

support in 1948. The next decade and a half saw economic policies that brought Czechoslovakia close to financial ruin, and an intolerance of non-communism that led to widespread persecution, and the deaths of thousands of people by execution.

'Prague Spring' & Charter 77

In the late 1960s, national Communist Party leader Alexander Dubček showed reformist colours through rapid liberalisation under the banner of 'socialism with a human face'. The Soviet regime crushed this 'Prague Spring' on the night of 20-21 August 1968 with Warsaw-Pact military hardware. In January 1977, a document called Charta 77 (Charter 77) was signed by nearly 250 intellectuals and artists, including Václav Havel – this public demand for basic human rights became an anti-communist tenet for dissidents.

National Velvet

A violent attack by police on hundreds of people attending a rally in Prague on 17 November 1989 generated continuous public demonstrations, culminating in 750,000 people gathering on Letná plain. A group led by Havel procured the government's resignation on 3 December, and 26 days later he was the new leader. This period of nonviolent demonstration became known as the Velvet Revolution. Peaceful 'problem-solving' was repeated when Slovak and Czech leaders agreed to go their separate ways on 1 January 1993, the day Prague became capital of the new Czech Republic and Havel its president.

New Independence

Subsequent years have unfortunately been marred by financial scandals and a highly unpopular power-sharing arrangement between the two main parties. Havel barely weathered the 1998 presidential elections, scraping in by a wafer-thin margin, and faces another in 2003.

Since the end of communism, Prague has seen a rise in crime and a deterioration in health and housing, though this has been partly compensated by a strengthened economy and an increasing deluge of tourist dollars.

ORIENTATION

Prague is situated on the Bohemian plateau and bisected by the country's longest river, the Vltava. The city is divided into 10 districts, each comprising a number of suburbs. The surprisingly compact historical centre (Praha 1) is itself subdivided into five distinct neighbourhoods. On the hill rising above the west bank of the Vltava is Hradčany (Castle District), which houses Prague's skyline-dominating main attraction. Immediately south is Malá Strana (Small Quarter), a charming 13th-century warren squeezed between the river and the large, leafy heights of Petřín Hill, and graced by the dome of St Nicholas Church.

On the east bank of the Vltava is Staré Město (Old Town), threaded with cobblestone streets and with its heart in the historic facades of Old Town Square. North of the Old Town is Josefov, the self-possessed Jewish quarter with a scattering of striking synagogues and mostly unhurried lanes. South of the Old Town (plus a smaller section to the north-east) is Nové Město (New Town), which contains the crowded commercialism of Wenceslas Square.

ENVIRONMENT

Traffic snarls are a major source of noxious irritation for anyone out for a walk in the late afternoon, particularly anywhere within breathing distance of Wenceslas Square. This, however, is nothing compared to the fume-laden haze that settles during the occasional winter inversions.

The Vltava has a less-than-pristine reputation when it comes to water quality, no-thanks to industrial pollution of the past and the increasing traffic plying the water in the name of tourism. But some fearless (or brainless) people have been spotted taking morning dips off Slovanský ostrov, and early evening on the riverbank off Josefov often finds someone with a line in the water.

Recycling is deeply imprinted on Czech domestic life, with large bins accepting paper, plastics and glassware in squares and other prominent locations. If staying in a private apartment in the Old Town, you may also be treated to a touch of noise pollution from late-night revellers or the ubiquitous municipal worker 'fixing' the paving just under your window.

Richard Nebesky

One of the many ferries that ply the Vltava waters

GOVERNMENT & POLITICS

Prague is the capital of the Czech Republic, a parliamentary democracy with a president (currently Václav Havel) chosen by parliament for a five-year term. The president in turn chooses the prime minister, who along with the cabinet *(vláda)* holds the real decision-making power. The parliament has a House of Representatives *(poslanecká sněmovna)* and a Senate *(sénat)*, both publicly elected.

Prague's governing body, the Local Government of the Capital City of Prague, has its seat elsewhere and is represented by a municipal office acting in concert with a mayor-headed council. The city contains 10 districts and 57 suburbs, each with their own district and local governments.

The Prague electorate has lately favoured the right-leaning Civic Democratic Party (ODS), in contrast to a national trend supporting the left-leaning Social Democrats (ČSSD), whose leader is current Prime Minister Miloš Zeman. But the political situation became unpredictable after a power-sharing deal between the two parties (ongoing) met with disapproval from President Havel and their supporters. The Communist party still has a dedicated core (albeit an elderly one) of supporters.

ECONOMY

The Czech Republic has been fighting back from a recession in 1999 and saw its economy grow by 2.5% in 2000. The majority of Prague's population are employed in one of the service industries, and a large proportion of those are connected in some way to the ever-growing local tourist industry. The swelling number of foreigners making the trip out to Prague contributes enormously to the local economy and obviously has a flow-on effect impacting the entire Czech Republic.

Unfortunately, many tourists are contributing too much due to the 'one price for them, one price for us' system applied by many establishments in the main tourist districts. This two-tiered pricing often results in visitors paying twice as much for their accommodation and entertainment as the local Czechs.

Roughly 10% of the population is employed in the manufacturing industry, specifically textiles, food and machinery. These activities take place mainly in the industrial suburbs of Smíchov and Karlín.

Did you Know?
- **Population** 1.2 million
- **Inflation** 3.8%
- **Unemployment** less than 2%
- **Average Czech monthly wage** 15,480Kč
- **Average price of pub beer** 10Kč/500mL

Richard Nebeský

SOCIETY & CULTURE

Czechs have a west Slavic background. The two main minority groups in Prague are Romany (gypsies) and Slovaks. There are also several sizeable expat communities, mainly contingents of Americans, Germans and Ukrainians; it's thought they make up about 4-5% of Prague's total population.

Czechs tend to be restrained socially, though they often let their hair down in the more popular beerhalls or non-tourist bars or restaurants. One of their strongest characteristics is a sense of humour, but it's hard to appreciate if you

'Nazdravi!' Toasting the day with a glass of local red

don't understand the language. Generally, the people of Prague are polite and mild-mannered – the few exceptions include life-or-death football fans, staff in some upmarket tourist places, and everybody who shops in the supermarket at Tesco. On a serious note, though admittedly rare, there have occasionally been reports of attacks by skin-heads on dark-skinned people.

Some common Czech civilities, which are also appreciated when uttered by visitors, include the following phrases: *dobrý den* (good morning); *dobrý večer* (good evening); *prosím* (please); *na shledanou* (goodbye); *nazdravi* (cheers); and *strč prst skrz krk* (stick your finger through your neck)… well, maybe not that last tongue-twister.

Etiquette

When attending most shows around town, you can rock up wearing pretty much anything you want (though couples wearing matching slacks and jackets should note such outfits violate international fashion laws). Operas, ballets and concerts at the larger or more traditional venues, however, are often attended by evening gowns and suits, usually with Czechs inside them.

Smoking is commonplace and there are few places that restrict or banish the activity, with obvious exceptions being inside public transport, museums, galleries and the like. It's the custom in many eateries to resist smoking over lunch, even if there are ashtrays on the table – if in doubt, ask a waiter.

Roma (Gypsies)

Roma or gypsies (*romové* or *cikáni*) are a minority group (0.3%) with a lineage that extends back to 15th-century India. They suffer neglect and hostility across the Czech Republic and Central Europe, due to a lack of acceptance of their generally closed, transient lifestyle; Roma involvement in petty theft and fraud in lieu of the unskilled blue-collar work they are normally restricted to; and, unfortunately, to flat-out racism.

The lack of Czech action to address the Roma's disproportionate levels of poverty, illiteracy and unemployment has been criticised by the EU in its assessment of Czech eligibility for EU membership.

ARTS
Architecture

The earliest architectural style you'll encounter in Prague is Romanesque (10th-12th centuries), featuring heavy stone walls with small windows; fine examples include the Basilica of St George and the Old Town Hall cellar. Gothic architecture (13th-16th centuries), built around ribbed vaults with high pointed arches, is exemplified by St Vitus' facade and the spindly heights of Týn Church. Renaissance architecture (15th-17th centuries) is classical, symmetrical, and often decorated with sgraffito (a multilayered mural technique), as at Schwarzenberg Palace on Hradcanské náměstí. The aggressively gaudy baroque approach (17th-18th centuries) is on display in St Nicholas Church in Malá Strana, and (unbelievably) led to an even more over-the-top style called rococo; see the fancy dress costume worn by Kinský Palace.

The revivalist period (late 18th-19th centuries) made the city like old, with resurrected styles applied to buildings like the neo-Renaissance National Theatre, while colourful Art Nouveau (circa 1899-1912) produced the exotic splendour of Municipal House. Also in the early 20th century, cubism appeared in structures like the House of the Black Madonna, after which Art Deco, plain-old functionalism and fantastically ugly communist residential blocks found their place in the city. The mixed styles post-1989 are hard to quantify but can be brilliantly original, such as in the form of the Dancing Building.

The hardcover *Prague – Eleven Centuries of Architecture* is a comprehensive guide to the city's design and is available in local bookshops.

Richard Nebesky

A mish-mash of styles and eras grace Prague's skyline.

Painting

The Czech Republic has a roll-call of prominent artists stretching back at least 600 years. Magister Theodoricus' painting impressed other Central European artists in the 14th century and can be seen in St Vitus' Chapel of St Wenceslas. Realism was a hit in the 19th century, with Mikuláš Aleš and the Mánes family leading the charge – and Josef was heavily influenced by romanticism.

Art Nouveau's patron saint was Alfons Mucha, whose back-catalogue is at the Mucha Museum. Famous impressionists of the same period included Max Švabinský and Antonín Slaviček. In the 20th century, an assortment of avant-garde and cubist artists, like Josef Čapek, made way for the surrealism of František Janoušek and later the socialist realism of Joseph Brož. The last few decades have seen artists making grotesquery brush strokes (Jiří Sopko) and fusing with electronic media (Woody Vašulka). The work of most of these artists is displayed at the Centre For Modern & Contemporary Art in Holešovice.

Literature

František Palacký's voluminous history of Bohemia and Moravia, the poems of Karel Hynek Mácha, and the romanticism of Božena Němcová were some of Czech literature's 19th-century standouts. Czech writers have a habit of becoming presidents: author and philosopher Tomáš Masaryk was Czechoslovakia's first leader, while current President Havel is a well-known scribe of plays and political commentary.

At the start of the 20th century, Franz Kafka wrote about his worst fears in *The Castle*, while Max Brod wrote about Kafka. Karel Čapek gave science fiction the robot treatment in *RUR* (Rossum's Universal Robots), and poet Jaroslav Seiffert's efforts pre-WWII eventually led to the Nobel Prize for Literature in 1984. Milan Kundera's books are well known internationally, as is the work of Ivan Klíma who wrote *The Ship Named Hope* and an excellent collection of essays, *The Spirit of Prague*. Bohumil Hrabal did a popular Garrison Keilor turn with *The Little Town That Stood Still*.

Cottage Kafka

Kafka may not have anticipated or much less desired it, but the man is a growth industry in Prague. Various venues either advertise a personal connection or invent an association. Places that were personally occupied by Kafka's stylised paranoia include his birthplace on the edge of Old Town Square (7, B4); Dum U minuty (7, D4), where he lived from 1889-96; the Little Blue Cottage (2, B4) in Golden Lane where he lived from 1916-17; and the venerable insurance office where he worked from 1908-22 (3, D11). Places that weren't, but wish they had been, include the Franz Kafka Café (7, A4), and an eponymous bookshop and a gallery (7, D5), both on Old Town Square.

Its claim to fame? 'Kafka lived here!'

Music

Traditional folk music prevailed in Bohemia and Moravia until after 950, when the Church tried to impose a Gregorian alternative. In the mid-19th century a crop of great composers emerged, among them Bedřich Smetana (1824-84), an advocate of the National Revival, and Antonín Dvořák (1841-1904), who produced fine chamber music and symphonies. Other notables were Leoš Janáček (1854-1928) and Jaroslav Ježek (1882-1969).

Prague has a deep-rooted jazz scene, with Czechs figuring prominently in European jazz circles until the 1948 communist coup d'état. The 1960s brought a less-censorial atmosphere and the appearance of Prague's first professional jazz club, Reduta (see p. 91). Names familiar to local aficionados include Jiřví Stivín and Milan Viklický. Czechs are no slouches on the rock/pop scene either, with a number of good (though often underground) bands pre-1989, and since then everything from hard rock and country & western to Roma classicists and obligatory pop specialists like Lucie Bílá.

highlights

There's a good reason why Unesco added Prague's historic centre to its World Cultural Heritage list in 1992, and it's not because the committee had too much of the flavoursome local beer. It's because Prague has some truly outstanding sights…like the hilltop magnificence of Prague Castle or the spires of Týn Church poking above the rooftops. And there's gotta be a reason all those people are swarming over Charles Bridge, right? But fortunately, there are just as many memorable sights that come in the form of a pleasant collision when you round that corner just up ahead.

Get up early one morning (ideally a Monday) and you'll find yourself wandering around with not much more than the occasional commuter or yawning tourist for company. This is the only time when places like Charles Bridge and the two main squares are empty enough for sweeping, undistracted gazes. And when exploring the Old Town, avoid the crowds beating a path through the narrow streets; with planning and a map, you can swing around the worst bottlenecks such as Karlova and explore some side-streets in the bargain.

Stopping Over

One Day Head straight to Old Town Square, swing around and let the architecture and crowds sink in. Cross Charles Bridge and climb to the imposing Prague Castle, where St Vitus Cathedral and the Garden on the Ramparts await. Stop at a beer-hall on Nerudova on the way back down, then grab dinner in the enigmatic lanes of Malá Strana.

Two Days Breakfast early on Národní, then ride the funicular up Petřín Hill. Walk across it to Strahov and the Loreta. Get a tram on Keplerova to Malostranská and then the subway to náměstí Republiky and Municipal House. Stroll the shops of Na Příkopě, peek at Wenceslas Square, then wine and dine around Pařížská.

Three Days Browse Havelská before getting to Josefov early to explore synagogues and the Old Jewish Cemetery. Take the metro to Vyšehrad for a relaxed wander around. Devote the evening to the nightspot-riddled streets behind the National Theatre.

Prague Lowlights

- Extortionate prices charged to foreigners
- Mid-winter smog attacks
- (Often) the chaos of Wenceslas Square and Charles Bridge
- Dodging tourist umbrellas in the Old Town
- Dumplings with the consistency of automobile putty
- Indifferent service
- Absinthe hangovers

Richard Nebesky

CENTRE FOR MODERN & CONTEMPORARY ART (4, D7)

The enormous Trade Fair Palace (Veletržní palác) in Holešovice harbours one of Prague's most stunning and rewardingly time-intensive art collections. Built in 1928 and at the time reputedly the largest building in the world, the 'palace' is an example of the so-called functionalist style, which from its rather unattractive exterior probably means it's meant to be functional, not aesthetic. Fortunately, the interior is an entirely different story.

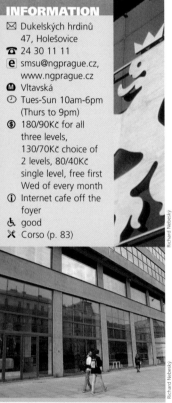

INFORMATION

- ✉ Dukelských hrdinů 47, Holešovice
- ☎ 24 30 11 11
- 📧 smsu@ngprague.cz, www.ngprague.cz
- Ⓜ Vltavská
- 🕐 Tues-Sun 10am-6pm (Thurs to 9pm)
- 💲 180/90Kč for all three levels, 130/70Kč choice of 2 levels, 80/40Kč single level, free first Wed of every month
- ⓘ Internet cafe off the foyer
- ♿ good
- 🍴 Corso (p. 83)

Richard Nebeský

Richard Nebeský

The gallery itself is no oil painting, but step inside and it's a different story.

There are three collections in the building, taking up the three highest levels (the ground floor hosts temporary exhibitions). On level 4 is mainly Czech **19th-century art** from artists such as Josef Mánes, pieces brimming with the imported neoclassicist leanings and early romanticism that dominated the time; there's also a German and Austrian section with a Klimt you won't want to miss. Level 3 has a small, very popular selection of **French 19th- and 20th-century art**, with work from Rodin, Monet and Picasso (OK, he was Spanish, but he worked in France); and a collection of **1900-30 art**, such as Cubist designs and early modern Czech sculpture. Level 2 has **1930-2000 art**, much of it surrealist and abstract material, plus space for Slovak art and changing exhibits from the youngest generation of Czech artists.

The only downside to this gallery is that there's so much to see. This is partly the intent of the curators, however, who don't just want to show visitors the art of a particular historical period, but to soak them in it. So take your time and have a long cultural bath.

DON'T MISS
- Josef Myslbek's soulful statue of Music • Josef Mánes' Josefina
- Art Deco furniture by Josef Gočár • Aleš Veselý's tortured *Enigmatic Objects* • Karel Pauzer's sublimely silly *Dog Family*

CHARLES BRIDGE (3, E3)

When a flood completely destroyed Judith Bridge in 1357, work began immediately on another bridge across the Vltava. The project was completed in 1402, and for the next 460-odd years Charles Bridge (Karlův most) was the only structure spanning the river. The 520m sandstone edifice was originally called (creatively) Stone Bridge, until it was bequeathed the name of its original commissioner, Charles IV, in 1870.

A common story told about the bridge's construction is that egg yolk was mixed into its mortar to make it sturdier – the weight-resistant qualities of egg yolk having obviously been well docu-

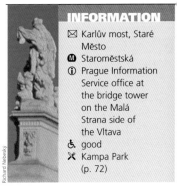

INFORMATION

✉ Karlův most, Staré Město
Ⓜ Staroměstská
ⓘ Prague Information Service office at the bridge tower on the Malá Strana side of the Vltava
♿ good
✗ Kampa Park (p. 72)

Richard Nebeský

mented – and that eggs were sent to Prague by helpful citizens from all over the region (apparently one particularly helpful town had them hard-boiled so they wouldn't break on the way).

Of the many interesting figures lining the bridge's sides, the first erected was the bronze **statue of St John of Nepomuk**, Czech patron saint, who was thrown into the Vltava by bad King Wenceslas IV in 1393. Other monuments include several of St Wenceslas, and one of St Christopher,

Seeing St John of Nepomuk can be a touching experience.

patron saint of travellers. The bridge was renovated in the 1970s and turned into a pedestrian zone.

Charles Bridge represents the best and worst of Prague. At its 'worst', it's sardine-packed with people elbowing, shouldering, ducking and weaving along its length; you can be so distracted getting across that you forget to actually look at the bridge or its magnificent view. The 'best' is a combination of the bridge's captivating physical form and the community feel that can often emanate from the collective of locals, foreigners and buskers who inhabit it.

DON'T MISS

• night-time view of a glowing Prague, with silhouetted statues in the foreground • standing on it at daybreak • carved decorations on Staré Město bridge tower

CHURCH OF OUR LADY BEFORE TÝN (7, C6)

Rising up behind the Týnská School (actually a parish school until the mid-19th century) is the hallowed mass of the Church of Our Lady Before Týn (Kostel Panny Marie Před Týnem), its exterior bristling with dramatic Gothic touches. The cathedral is an Old Town Square landmark with distinctive twin spires that are a reassuring sight to many tourists after losing their bearings (again) in the narrow surrounding byways.

INFORMATION

- ✉ Staroměstské náměstí, Staré Město
- Ⓜ Staroměstská; Můstek
- ⊘ services Mon-Fri 4.30pm, Sat 1pm, Sun 11.30am & 9pm
- ⑤ free
- ⓘ occasional concerts
- ⚬ good (entry from Celetná)
- ✗ Ebel Coffee House (p. 79)

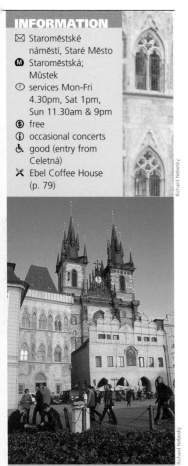

Richard Nebeský

Richard Nebeský

Týn: all flash and treasure

Construction on Týn Church began in 1380 to replace another chapel, but the building contract apparently didn't specify an end date, as subsequent years saw the completion of items such as the roof (1457), gable (1463), southern tower (1511), and a new northern tower (1835).

The church was initially a stronghold of Hussitism, the church-reform movement championed by Jan Hus in the late 14th and early 15th centuries, but eventually succumbed to Catholicism and the lavish worship of baroque interior design.

Anyone unaccustomed to the sheer immodesty of baroque decor should be warned that the first glimpse of the Church of Our Lady Before Týn's massive interior, replete with imposing statuary and incredibly ornate altars, will probably come as something of a visual shock.

People sometimes circumnavigate the church puzzling over where to find the correct entry – you'll be able to access it at the far end of the passageway that opens up beside Café Italia on the Old Town Square.

- tomb of Tycho Brahe ● rococo altar at northern end ● Karel Škretäs' altar artwork ● the sound of the renovated 17th-century pipe organ during concerts

LORETA   (5, B3)

The Loreta is a significant and splendid pilgrimage site established by Baroness Benigna Katharina von Lobkowicz in 1626 and subsequently maintained and protected by the Capuchins, an order associated with St Francis of Assisi's brotherhood. Its spiritual centrepiece is a replica of **Santa Casa**, the house of the Virgin Mary in Palestine that stood in Nazareth before being dismantled by pilgrims and shipped to Loreto in Italy in 1294.

Legend has it that angels provided the transportation, but this could have something to do with the name of the family who patronised the house-moving – Angeli.

The Santa Casa copy, complete with original fresco fragments and the wonder-working statue (its actual name) of Our Lady of Loreto, sits in a fine courtyard surrounded by chapel-lined arcades. The **Church of the Nativity of Our Lord** has a deliriously baroque altar, a rococo organ and some beautiful frescos; the side altars of **Sts Felicissimus and Marcia** contain the aristocratically dressed remains of two Spanish martyrs. In the south-western corner is the **Chapel of Our Lady of Sorrows**, which has a sculpture of a crucified bearded woman – apparently St Starosta successfully prayed for a beard to maintain her chastity, but her father had her crucified for thus screwing up her arranged marriage.

Tours end with a glimpse inside **Loreto Treasury** and its breathtaking display of pilgrim- and patron-donated riches, including a wonderful altar made of ebony. If you need a breath of air after gazing at this lot, wander over to the scenic terraces beside Strahov Monastery.

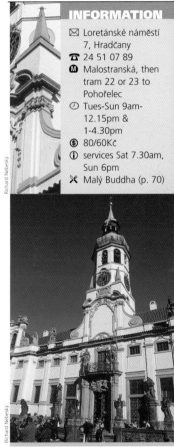

INFORMATION

- ⊠ Loretánské náměstí 7, Hradčany
- ☎ 24 51 07 89
- Ⓜ Malostranská, then tram 22 or 23 to Pohořelec
- ⏱ Tues-Sun 9am-12.15pm & 1-4.30pm
- Ⓢ 80/60Kč
- ⓘ services Sat 7.30am, Sun 6pm
- ✗ Malý Buddha (p. 70)

Richard Nebeský

Richard Nebeský

Have angels, will travel

DON'T MISS
- 'Prague Sun' monstrance and its 6000-plus diamonds in the Treasury
- 27-bell carillon at entrance playing on the hour • *Presentation in the Temple* fresco in Church of the Nativity of Our Lord

MUNICIPAL HOUSE   (7, C10)

Few buildings in Prague can elicit the delight that many visitors feel when they first lay their eyes on the exuberant facade of Municipal House (Obecní Dům). The building opened in 1912 on the site of King's Court, the official Bohemian monarch's residence from the late 14th century until the Hapsburgs moved into the area in 1526. It was intended to be suitably impressive as the architectural representative of Prague, and so a collective of well-credentialled painters and sculptors were commissioned to create an Art Nouveau masterpiece; among the famous names who contributed were Alfons Mucha, Karel Špillar, Josef Myslbek and Bohumil Kafka.

INFORMATION

✉ náměstí Republiky 5, Staré Město
☎ 22 00 21 00
🖳 www.obecni-dum.cz
Ⓜ Náměstí Republiky
🕘 7.30am-11pm
⑤ guided tours 150Kč
ⓘ guided tours from information centre (open 10am-6pm); classical concerts in Smetana Hall
♿ good
✗ Kavárna obecní dům (p. 76)

Richard Nebeský

Richard Nebeský

Home is where the art is.

While the facade is amazing enough, festooned as it is with sculpted allegorical figures, taking centre stage inside (literally) is the biggest concert hall in town, **Smetana Hall**, dripping with frescos, sculptures and natural light from the original skylights. **Mayor Hall** is where Mucha left his brushstrokes, most of them on the ceiling fresco *Slavic Concorde*, which depicts an eagle metaphorically held aloft by Czech-personified human virtues. Not content with painting, Mucha also designed the doorway curtains and windowpanes.

If you feel like some sustenance at either of the two ground-level eateries, don't expect any respite from the grand decor. Both the upmarket **Francouzská Restaurace** (see p. 79) and the more casual *kavárna* (cafe; see p. 76) are decked out as sumptuously as anywhere else.

DON'T MISS
● Josef Pekárek's Nymph fountain on the cafe's front wall ● ceramic wainscoting lining the stairwell to the basement ● original pool hall off the cafe ● the Prague Symphony Orchestra in Smetana Hall (p. 95)

MUSEUM OF DECORATIVE ARTS   (3, C5)

Home renovators in need of a few classic ideas may want to head for the neo-Renaissance building across the road from the Rudolfinum, where there's a fabulous historical catalogue of 16th- to early-20th-century domestic decorations. The Museum of Decorative Arts (Umělecko-Průmyslové Muzeum) was set up here in 1900 in an effort to spur on local ambition for the region's often-criticised applied arts scene, which had become dominated by Industrial Revolution blandness. The museum has now amassed over 250,000 exemplary pieces, though you'll find only a fraction of these are on display here.

Above reception is a hall for **temporary exhibitions** which are often well worth a look; a popular previous display featured wares from the

Richard Nebeský

INFORMATION

✉ 17.listopadu 2, Josefov
☎ 51 09 31 11
@ direct@upm-praha.anet.cz
Ⓜ Staroměstská
🕐 Tues 10am-8pm, Wed-Sun 10am-6pm
$ 80/30Kč, children up to 10 free
ⓘ free audio guides; reference library of creative arts (☎ 232 84 72, @ www.knihovna.upm.cz)
♿ good
✕ Espresso

International Glass Symposium. But the main reason for visiting is the permanent top-floor exhibit called **The Story of Materials**. Though a fairly uninspiring title, the exhibition is anything but, with fascinating displays of tapestries and secular/liturgical clothing ('Fibre'); old photos, graphics and some massive, intricately-bound tomes ('Print & Picture'); and ceramic and glassware artefacts ('Art of Fire').

As if that isn't enough, the **Treasure Hall** has a beautiful selection of raw materials and furniture. Time will tell if the planned section on clocks makes an appearance.

Head inside for a knick-knack attack.

DON'T MISS
• display of decorative copes & chasubles • inlaid & carved 1740 longcase clock • exquisite cabinets in Treasure Hall • stairwell ceiling & stained-glass windows

NATIONAL MUSEUM (3, K11)

The neo-Renaissance bulk of the National Museum (Národní Muzeum), with its staggering **natural history collection**, commands the southern end of Wenceslas Square. Established as the Patriotic Museum by aristocrats including the naturalist Kaspar Sternberg in 1818, the museum had a restless childhood that included a stint in Sternberg Palace in Hradčany before moving to a site on Na příkopě in 1846, and finally settling on its current spot in 1891.

The cavernous interior of the museum has wall-to-wall displays of earthly magnificence, from a zoology section with more stuffed animals than a Disney store, to some distinctly unreal creatures mounted in entomology department cases, as well as the palaeontology section's big-boned residents. Kids especially will get a kick out of the reconstructed Fin whale and the shockingly large crustaceans in a small display case on the top floor. It's a shame, though, that the museum's wealth of natural resources is presented in such a monotonously static way; the mineralogy section is particularly enthusiasm-sapping, with row upon row of cabinets with Czech labels (there is an audio guide, though it costs double the standard admission).

If you need some man-made splendour to refocus your attention, sit for a while in the stunning **main stairwell**. Or practise your stand-up material in front of the captive audience in the **Pantheon**, with its statues of prominent secular Czech citizens and upper-level murals.

INFORMATION

- ⊠ Václavské náměstí 68, Nové Město
- ☎ 24 49 71 11, 24 49 72 12
- e www.nm.cz
- Ⓜ Muzeum
- ☉ May-Sept: 10am-6pm; Oct-Apr: 9am-5pm; closed first Tues of every month
- Ⓢ 70/35Kč, children under 6 free; free first Mon of every month
- ⓘ audio guides 145/100Kč
- ♿ good
- ✕ on-site cafe

Richard Nebesky

The Pantheon puts on a good floor show

Unnatural Selection

The natural history collection has occasionally been an unorthodox target during times of conflict. In May 1945, one day before Germany resigned from WWII, a German flying bomb hit the building and destroyed several collections. Then in August 1968, Warsaw Pact soldiers mysteriously riddled the museum's exterior with bullets – you can still see the scars in the sandstone facade.

NATIONAL THEATRE   (3, J4)

One of Prague's more eye-catching buildings is the National Theatre (Národní Divadlo), particularly on a bright day when reflected sunlight blazes from the metal-sheathed roof – but it means a lot more to Czech people than a landmark. The building emerged out of a cultural and political climate in the late 19th century that demanded mainstream presentation of Czech theatre, not just because no other large venue existed, but also because the idea embodied the ubiquitous nationalistic spirit of the time. Backed by notables such as historian František Palacký and composer Bedřich Smetana, and designed by Josef Zítek, the theatre came to life in 1881 – only to promptly burn down. It reopened two years later.

The building's internal and external decorations were the work of a number of well-known Czech artists, who achieved such prestige from their work that thereafter they were known as the 'National Theatre Generation'. The prominent chariots on top of pillars to one side of the main entry were the handiwork of Ladislav Šaloun, while creators of the foyer busts included Josef Myslbek and Jan Štursa.

Reward yourself before or after a performance as Czech patrons used to do with a coffee at **Kavárna Slavia** (see p. 76) across the road, though note that this one-time intellectual and dissident hangout is now a more commercial venue.

INFORMATION

- ✉ Národní 2, Nové Město
- ☎ 24 90 14 48
- e www.narodni-divad lo.cz
- Ⓜ Národní Třída
- ⓘ box office Mon-Fri 10am-6pm, Sat-Sun 10am-12.30pm & 3pm-6pm
- ♿ good
- ✗ Dynamo (p. 75)

Richard Nebesky

Richard Nebesky

Familiar Sounds

When the National Theatre reopened on 18 November 1883 after suffering a devastating fire two years earlier, it did so to the strains of Bedrich Smetana's opera *Libuše*. In a nice bit of cultural synergy, the theatre reopened again exactly one century later (this time after six years of intensive restoration) to the same opera.

Getting in on the act

OLD-NEW SYNAGOGUE (3, C6)

The Old-New Synagogue (Staronová Synagóga) is the oldest synagogue in Europe, erected in Gothic style in the late 13th century to serve as Prague's

INFORMATION

- ⊠ Červená, Josefov
- Ⓜ Staroměstská
- ⏱ Apr-Oct: Sun-Thurs
  9.30am-6pm, Fri
  9.30am-5pm; Nov-
  Mar: Sun-Thurs
  9.30am-5pm, Fri
  9.30am-2pm;
  closed on Jewish
  holidays
- ⑤ 200/140Kč
- ① guides included in
  admission
- ✗ Jeruzalem (p. 71)

Richard Nebesky

prime site of Jewish worship. Jews are thought to have settled in the city as early as the mid-10th century, though an area known as Jewish Town (later **Josefov**; see p. 40) was not established until around 200 years later. Originally called the New or Great Shul, and subsequently labelled 'Old-New' once other synagogues appeared, the building on Červená is believed to have been predated by an important synagogue called Old Shul, which was torn down in 1867. The site of Old Shul is now occupied by the Moorish splendour of the **Spanish Synagogue** (see p. 40).

The Old-New Synagogue, which underwent restoration in 1998-9, has the twin naves typical of secular and sacred medieval architecture, and a half-dozen bays with ribbed vaulting. On the eastern wall is the **holy ark** in which the Torah scrolls are kept, with a wonderful grapevine-carved **tympanum** above it. In the centre of the synagogue is the bimah (raised platform supporting a pulpit), enclosed by a 15th-century iron grille, and on the walls are Hebrew biblical abbreviations.

Remember that if you want to enter the synagogue, men must have their heads covered – yarmulkes are handed out at the entrance, though hats or bandannas are allowable substitutions.

The Legend of Golem

The many prominent rabbis who have spoken here have included Rabbi Loew. Legend has it that Loew fashioned a living creature from clay – Golem – to help stop the local persecution of Jews. After deciding Golem had fulfilled his original mission, Loew apparently 'undid' his creation in the loft of the Old-New Synagogue, where the now-lifeless clay figure reputedly still lies.

Good help is hard to find…

OLD TOWN HALL & ASTRONOMICAL CLOCK (7, C5)

The 1338 **Town Hall** of Staré Město (Staroměstská Radnice) is a complex of local homes that were incorporated and rebuilt over many years. One of the most famous is at the Malé náměstí end: the sgraffito-covered building that once housed a young Franz Kafka.

Perched on the tower is the beautifully styled **Astronomical Clock**, a 1490 device with an upper face graced with representations of astronomical movement and external figurines joined on the hour by a parade of apostles for a brief and extremely popular mechanical show.

Inside, most visitors charge straight for the 60m **tower**, which offers an excellent perspective on the mosaic of people in the square below. On the first floor is the Gothic **chapel** and the **Hall of the Mayors of the City**. The chapel was consecrated in 1381 in the names of Czech patron saints Wenceslas, Vitus and Ludmila, and has a lovely oriel colourfully streaked by stained-glass. The Hall of Mayors is as dry as it sounds, with a collection of portraits of mainly 18th-century civic chiefs. Accessible from the ground floor are the newly reconstructed Romanesque and Gothic **historic halls**.

Though huge crowds gather to watch the clock go through its paces, it's not quite the spectacle you might be led to believe – fun, yes, but quick and unspectacular. Catch it from the crowd perimeter, but getting stuck in the throng that gathers 15 minutes before each performance is a less-than-rewarding experience.

INFORMATION

- ✉ Staroměstské náměstí 1, Staré Město
- ☎ 124 44
- Ⓜ Staroměstská; Můstek
- ⏰ Apr-Oct: Mon 11am-6pm, Tues-Sun 9am-6pm; Nov-Mar: Mon 11am-5pm, Tues-Sun 9am-5pm
- 💲 30/20Kč (separate tickets required for each of the following: historical halls, Gothic chapel and tower)
- ⓘ on-site PIS conducts guided tours
- ♿ good
- ✗ Country Life (p. 78)

Chris Mellor

Chris Mellor

Clocking in for a timeless attraction

DON'T MISS
- view of clock's apostles from Gothic chapel • original Mánes-painted calendar wheel at Museum of the City of Prague (p. 34)
- gawking at the size of the crowd gawking at the clock

OLD TOWN SQUARE (7, C5)

The geographical hub of the Old Town, Staroměstské Náměstí, is also one of the tourist hubs of Prague. On any given day, regardless of the weather

or time (except early morning), you'll find people streaming across the paving from every direction to take seats at the overpriced outdoor restaurants and bars, mass patiently in front of the **Astronomical Clock** (see p. 23), or sit on benches around the **statue of Jan Hus** (see p. 37) to puff on cigarettes or assess the latest footage on hand-held videos.

Sometimes called Staromák, the square became Prague's central marketplace in the late 12th century, taking the commercial baton from a marketplace that was sited where the thoroughfare of Široká is today. This job description lasted for over seven centuries, in which time a plethora of architectural styles found homes around the

square's perimeter. Some of the most prominent examples include the Gothic **Church of Our Lady Before Týn** (see p. 16); the marvellous late baroque-constructed but rococo-swathed **Kinský Palace** (see p. 36); the **House of the Stone Bell** (see p. 35), with its Gothic facade underneath a pastel baroque facing; and, on the southern side of the square, the gay neo-Renaissance frontage of **Štorch House**.

A Date With History

1338	John of Luxembourg gives OK for town hall
1422	Hussite preacher Jan Želivský executed
1458	Hussite George of Poděbrady elected King of Bohemia
1915	6 July – Statue of 500-year-old martyr Hus unveiled
1945	8 May – Withdrawing German troops try to wreck town hall
1948	21 February – Communist government proclaimed from Kinský balcony
1968	21 August – Warsaw Pact tanks end 'Prague Spring'

PETŘÍN HILL (2, G2)

Glorious though Prague's historic streets may be, sometimes there's nothing like some greenery, and I'm not talking about what's occasionally offered by passersby on the Royal Way. Petřín Hill (Petřínské Sady) is the large mound providing a natural backdrop to Malá Strana, and is an excellent place to play with the kids, read a book, or just wander the leafy trails that crisscross its surface.

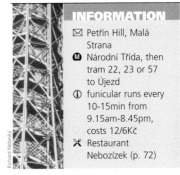

INFORMATION

✉ Petřín Hill, Malá Strana

Ⓜ Národní Třída, then tram 22, 23 or 57 to Újezd

ⓘ funicular runs every 10-15min from 9.15am-8.45pm, costs 12/6Kč

✗ Restaurant Nebozízek (p. 72)

If you've chosen to ride the **funicular** (see p. 110) up from Újezd, you can either disembark halfway up the 318m hill or head to the terminus, where the 299 steps of **Petřín Tower** await. This 62m tower is a scale model (5:1) of the Eiffel Tower, built in 1891 for the Prague Exposition, and has spectacular views to accompany your gasping and snorting. Nearby, the kiddies (or more mature juveniles) will love distorting themselves in the **Maze** (see p. 45), or scoping out the **Štefánik Observatory**.

Sometimes even the crowds up here can get to you. If you feel the onset of social exhaustion, follow the old fortifications south-east and head through the wall to the southern side of the hill. Here in peaceful **Kinský Gardens** you'll find lots of places to relax, and not too far in is the unique construction of the **Church of St Michael** (see p. 39).

Food for fort: the Hunger Wall, built by paupers in return for food

DON'T MISS • walking along the Hunger Wall • Church of St Lawrence's ceiling fresco • stopping to take in city views • letting yourself get lost

PRAGUE CASTLE (2, C4)

Every city usually has several places clamouring to be rated *the* major draw-card, but in Prague there's no argument. With its magnificent clifftop outlook, an 1100-year history going back to a simple walled-in compound in the 9th century, and a breathtaking scale that qualifies it as the biggest ancient castle in the world, Prague Castle (Pražský Hrad) is the indisputable centrepiece of the Czech capital.

INFORMATION

- ✉ Hradčany
- ☎ 24 37 33 68, 24 37 24 34
- 🌐 www.hrad.cz
- Ⓜ Malostranská; Hradčanská
- ⏲ historic buildings Apr-Oct 9am-5pm, Nov-Mar 9am-4pm; grounds Apr-Oct 5am-midnight, Nov-Mar 6am-11pm
- ⓢ 120/60/180Kč for 3-day ticket to Castle highlights; grounds free admission
- ⓘ information centre open Apr-Oct 9am-5pm, Nov-Mar 9am-4pm; audio guide 145/180Kč 2/3hrs; guided tours Tues-Sun 9am-4pm 80Kč
- ♿ good
- ✗ Café Poet (p. 70)

Richard Nebeský

Richard Nebeský

Richard Nebeský

The lights are on, but Havel's not home!

The castle has undergone regular renovations since the first fortifications went up, starting in the 12th century with the Romanesque features added by Prince Sobeslav I, through to the mid-16th century planting of the **Royal Garden** (see p. 41) and construction of the Renaissance **Royal Summer Palace** (see p. 36) then up to and beyond the consecration of **St Vitus Cathedral** (see p. 29) in 1929. It remains the Czech seat of power and official residence of the president, though current big cheese Václav Havel has chosen to live elsewhere – probably something to do with the lack of parking and street noise.

Parts of the palace that visitors flock to include the main gate on **Hradčanské náměstí** (see p. 42) where a regimented changing of the guards happens on the hour, the unmissable Czech history exhibition in **Lobkowicz Palace** (see p. 33), the **Basilica of St George** (see p. 39), and the collection of Bohemian art in the **Convent of St George** (see p. 35). Other worthwhile sections include the **Toy Museum** (see p. 46), though the static displays need patience, and the immensely pleasurable atmosphere of the **Garden on the Ramparts** (see p. 41).

DON'T MISS • cottages of Golden Lane • excellent exhibitions at Prague Castle Gallery • following marching soldiers as their leader clears a path through crowds by clattering his rifle butt on the stones

ST NICHOLAS CHURCH (2, D4)

There are three churches called St Nicholas in Prague, but only one that took 82 years and three generations of one family to build, and is regarded as an outstanding example of baroque architecture. This is the St Nicholas Church (Kostel Sv Mikuláše) located west of the Vltava that has greedily consumed most of the available space in Malostranské náměstí, and as an encore dominates the local skyline with its 70m-high verdigris dome. Work on the church was started by a Jesuit order in 1673, but it was a Dientzenhofer father-son act, plus a next generation son-in-law, who were directly responsible for the construction of the church, finally finished in 1755.

The incredible late-baroque interior contains numerous pillars, frescoes and life-size sculptures. One of the artists who had a hand in the 10 years' worth of interior decorating was Karel Škréta, who produced a painting for the chapel's main altar; you should find a small collection of some of his dark, glowering paintings in the **upstairs gallery**. Speaking of hands, Mozart ran his over the 2500-pipe organ in 1787, and was rewarded with a Requiem mass here after his death. If you're not feeling too giddy from the ornamentation, you can also climb the **bell tower** for an extra fee.

INFORMATION

✉ Malostranské náměstí 38, Malá Strana

Ⓜ Malostranská

🕐 9am-4.30pm; belfry Apr-Oct 10am-6pm (ticket sales end 5.30pm), Nov-Mar: Sat-Sun 10am-5pm

$ 45/20Kč, belfry 30/20Kč

ⓘ concerts usually held 5pm

✗ U tří zlatých hvězd (p. 74)

Art Imitates Roof

The enormous ceiling fresco, *Apotheosis of St Nicholas* by Johann Lucas Kracker, is the largest in Europe. To check out its other claim to fame, head up to the gallery and look at how the painting has been skilfully rendered to blend near-perfectly with the ceiling architecture, so the two are practically inseparable.

Richard Nebeský

The story of St Nick told in pictures

STRAHOV MONASTERY (5, D2)

The giant white Strahov Monastery (Strahovský Klášter) looks down from its Petřín Hill vantage point over the densest part of Malá Strana, a serene view which gives its grounds an extra-meditative quality. The monastery was established in 1140 by Prince Vladislav II for the Premonstratensians, followers of the teachings of St Augustine, but the complex didn't undergo its most significant developments (including the reconstruction of a brewery) until the 17th and 18th centuries.

The highlight of a visit to Strahov, apart from the inherent pleasure in just getting to its delightful location, is its **library**, comprising one of the oldest monastic collections in the country. Researchers get access to many of the age-bleached books and manuscripts. Others have to be content with glimpses of the 50,000 tomes in the baroque, double-storey Philosophy Hall, built in 1794 and decorated with a fresco by Anton Maulbertsch, and the 16,000 books of the equally stunning Theology Hall. The **gallery** (see p. 36) has a fascinating collection of monastic paintings and sculptures from Bohemia and elsewhere in Europe, including early-19th-century Czech masters and Dutch, Flemish and Italian 17th-18th-century painters.

If you've yet to have your fill of weighty baroque, have a look at the interior of the **Church of the Assumption of Our Lady**, built in 1143. There's also a **Museum of Czech Literature** here, though the inherently interesting assorted manuscripts, photos and other displays don't make a lot of sense unless you can understand Czech.

INFORMATION

- ✉ Strahovské nádvoří 1, Strahov
- ☎ library 20 51 66 71, museum 24 51 11 37
- Ⓜ Malostranská, then tram 22 or 23 to Pohořelec
- ⊘ library 9am-noon & 1-5pm, museum Tues-Sun 9am-5pm, gallery Tues-Sun 9am-noon & 12.30-5pm
- ⑤ library 50/30Kč, museum 30/15Kč, gallery 35K/20č
- ⓘ library viewed by tour only
- ✗ Oživlé Dřevo (p. 70)

Richard Nebesky

Strahov, the perfect place to ruminate, meditate, illuminate, appreciate...

Richard Nebesky

DON'T MISS
- 9th-century jewel-encrusted Strahov gospel (library) • the staff of Jeroným II, former Strahov abbot (gallery) • being confused by the preserved fruit & weird sea creatures in the 'Dept of Curiosities'

ST VITUS CATHEDRAL (2, C3)

St Vitus Cathedral (Katedrála Sv Vita) towers above the third courtyard of Prague Castle, primed to use its enormous Gothic stature to intimidate first-time visitors wandering innocently in from the main gate. Equipped with a lofty 100m main tower, this is the largest cathedral in the Czech Republic, a fact that helps explain why it took centuries to get this awesome beast from the drawing board to reality. King Charles IV initiated its construction in 1344 on the site of a 10th-century rotunda, but it wasn't until thousands of pieces of glass had been painstakingly set in the large west-facing rose window in 1929 that St Vitus was finally finished.

The cathedral's enormous nave is encircled by side-chapels, the most striking of which is the **Chapel of St Wenceslas** with its precious, glittering stonework. Not to be outdone, though, is the **tombstone of St John of Nepomuk**, which is so stupefyingly overwrought that it's hard to believe anyone could be sombre around it. Beneath the floor of the cathedral is the **Royal Crypt**, a claustrophobic space (particularly when jammed with fellow visitors) with a view to the stately sarcophagi of Charles IV, Wenceslas IV, Rudolf II and George of Poděbrady. You should rightly be tempted to scale the **tower** for the great views at the top, but be prepared for 287 slow, strenuous steps.

INFORMATION

- ✉ Prague Castle, Hradčany
- ☎ 24 37 33 68 (castle information centre)
- e www.hrad.cz
- Ⓜ Malostranská; Hradčanská
- ⊘ Apr-Oct: 9am-5pm; Nov-Mar: 9am-4pm
- ⑤ 120/60/180Kč for 3-day ticket giving full access to Castle highlights
- ⓘ information centre Apr-Oct 9am-5pm, Nov-Mar 9am-4pm; audio guide 145/180Kč 2/3hrs; guided tours Tues-Sun 9am-4pm 80Kč
- ♿ good
- ✗ U Zlaté studné (p. 72)

Stained In Style

St Vitus Cathedral is blessed with some exemplary stained-glass windows, produced by local artisans over a 100-year period. For some of the oldest examples, see the three windows in the Chapel of St Antony (1865-6); for one of the newest, see the window in the southern wall of the Chapel of St Wenceslas (1968). For information on all of St Vitus's glasswork, buy the book *The Windows of St Vitus's Cathedral* from the Museum Shop.

VYŠEHRAD (4, E7)

Visit Vyšehrad to soak up the atmosphere of an old fortified site surrounded by legends linking it to the birth of Prague, or to stroll through the extensive **gardens** (see p. 42) and enjoy excellent views of inactivity down on the Vltava. Either way, the trip to this historic battlement from the town centre takes just a swift metro ride followed by a short walk.

In the late 11th century, King Vratislav II chose Vyšehrad as the site for a palace, the Church of Sts Peter and Paul, and what is now the city's oldest Romanesque structure, **St Martin Rotunda**. But the subsequent rise of Prague Castle as the royal seat meant the decline of this southern stronghold. Charles IV resurrected Vyšehrad with a Gothic palace, but the Hussite wars wiped it out. After a stint as an army garrison, the now-baroque fortress landed in the in-tray of city officials in the 1920s and has since been a quiet, historic park.

The fresco-covered interior of the **Church of Sts Peter and Paul** is worth a look, as are the casemates inside the ramparts – from Brick Gate you can enter Gorlice Hall,

INFORMATION

- ✉ Soběslavova 2, Vyšehrad
- ☎ 24 92 07 35, 24 91 99 39
- Ⓜ Vyšehrad
- ⊘ Apr-Oct 9.30am-6pm, Nov-Mar 9.30am-5pm
- Ⓢ grounds free; Church of Sts Peter & Paul 15/5Kč
- ① information centre just beyond Tábor Gate, approached from the metro station
- Ⓖ good
- ✗ Na Vyšehradé

Richard Nebeský

Richard Nebeský

A doorway to an ancient world

where four of Charles Bridge's original statues are kept. Of special significance to Czechs is **Vyšehrad Cemetery**, containing the graves of well-known countryfolk like Dvořák, Smetana, Mucha and Čapek.

Stuff of Legends

Czech legends attempt to explain the birth of Prague in mythological terms, most (it's been theorised) constructed in the minds of social chroniclers. Vyšehrad features heavily in these stories, and this legendary status has made the old fortress a magnet for poets, painters and composers, particularly those who were working during the 19th-century resurgence of Czech culture (Czech National Revival) and sought an enigmatic icon to represent the Czech past.

WENCESLAS SQUARE (3, J10)

Wenceslas Square (Václavské Náměstí) is a commerce-frenzied arena full of pitched battles between shoppers looking for a good deal and proprietors looking for profit. It's also the rallying point for tourists desperate to walk in a straight line after weaving through the arabesque streets of the Old Town, and for members of the Prague populace working nearby or just looking for a place to hang out. It's one of the busiest places in the city and not the place to go if you're feeling a tad jaded with crowds, particularly during commuter rush hours.

INFORMATION
- ✉ Václavské náměstí, Nové Město
- Ⓜ Můstek; Muzeum
- ♿ good
- ✖ Branický sklípek (p. 75)

The square has always had commerce on its mind, serving its apprenticeship as a medieval horse market. It received its name during the democratic revolution of 1848 and cemented its historical prominence as a public space by being the scene of independence protests in 1918, and of attempts to block advancing Russian military in 1968. In 1969, a student called Jan Palach famously protested the Warsaw Pact invasion by setting fire to himself and collapsing under the large **statue of Wenceslas**.

Palach's suffering and that of other people under communism is commemorated by a simple **memorial** near the statue. Stand-out buildings around the square include the **National Museum** (see p. 20), the faded Art Nouveau grandeur of **Hotel Europa** (see p. 104), and the **Melantrich Building**, where Havel and Alexander Dubček spoke from the balcony in 1989.

King and commoner alike hang out at Wenceslas.

DON'T MISS
- exploring the shops in Lucerna Passage (p. 43) ● neo-Renaissance murals on Wiehl House ● disappearing into Františkánská zahrada (p. 41) ● having a coffee in the worn-out Café Europa

sights & activities

Prague's many attractions refuse to huddle together and instead reside all over the inner city and in outward-bound areas. This gives you the chance to explore an invigorating spread of neighbourhoods while pounding the pavements between historically resplendent squares and streets, majestic church-fronts, green open-air cuttings, and ticket booths.

Neighbourhoods

Prague's cherished past is served up for tourist consumption in **Staré Město** (Old Town), stretching from the Vltava east to náměstí Republiky, north to Široká and Dlouhá, and south to Národní, 28.října and Na Příkopě. Northwards is **Josefov**, centre of Prague's Jewish community, with some flash hotels, and upmarket cafes on Pařížská. South and east of the Old Town lies **Nové Město** (New Town), a commercial area with more recent historical attractions, plus lively clubs, bars and restaurants west of Wenceslas Square.

Vinohrady, south-east of the main train station, is the brash newcomer, stuffed with trendy eateries and watering holes that service the local high-flyers. Staring at it bemusedly from the north is **Žižkov**, an edgy industrial suburb with new alternative-scene credentials. South of New Town is Prague's ethereal second castle, **Vyšehrad**, and across the river is another grunge-infested industrial enclave, **Smíchov**. Directly north sits **Malá Strana** (Small Quarter), where beautiful people walk their dogs through some of the city's most picturesque streets.

Further north are the heights of **Hradčany**, where the spectacular castle lives. North-east of here, on the Vltava's 'big bend', is the parkland swathe of **Letná**, which is bordered in the north-west by a one-time fishing village that now features parks and residential areas, **Bubeneč**. Finally, in the north-east, you'll enjoy an eclectic mix of fairgrounds, galleries and cheap accommodation in **Holešovice**.

Off the Beaten Track

'Getting away from it all' in Prague is difficult because it means getting away from yourself, the visitor. It can be done, though, and often it's just a case of a short metro and/or tram ride.

Try the still, leafy grounds of **Vyšehrad** (p. 30) for a quick trip that can feel like a weekend away. Or use the **Church of St Michael** (p. 39) as an excuse to recline on the south side of Petřín Hill. Alternatively, climb the 299 steps of **Petřín Tower** (see pic right) for a spectacular view. The **Lapidárium** (p. 33) is a stony treat, while a glimpse of **Church of the Most Sacred Heart of Our Lord** (p. 39) can become an investigation of sophisticated Vinohrady or the back-blocks of real-life Žižkov.

MUSEUMS

Ceremonial Hall (3, C5)
Formerly the Old Jewish Cemetery mortuary (see p. 38) and now part of the Jewish Museum, the Ceremonial Hall (Obřadní Síň) is the site of an interesting exhibition on Jewish traditions relating mainly to illness and death; the rest of the exhibit is next door in Klaus Synagogue.
✉ U starého hřbitova 3a, Josefov ☎ 22 31 71 91 e office@jewish museum.cz; www.jewish museum.cz Ⓜ Staroměstská ☺ Nov-Mar: Sun-Fri 9am-4pm; Apr-Oct: Sun-Fri 9am-6pm; closed Jewish holidays Ⓢ Jewish Museum 290/200Kč

Czech Museum of Fine Arts (7, C8)
Behind the cubist facade of the House of the Black Madonna is, fittingly, a fine arts museum (České Muzeum Výtvarných Umění) with outstanding examples of Czech cubism. Direct from 1911-19 are cubist sculptures, paintings and furniture (including the world's most uncomfortable couch), and a stairwell railing resembling a mini-rollercoaster. There's another gallery at Husova 19-21.
✉ Celetná 34, Staré Město ☎ 24 21 17 32; Husova branch 22 22 02 18 Ⓜ Náměstí Republiky ☺ Tues-Sun 10am-6pm Ⓢ 35/15Kč ⓰

Jewish Museum (3, C5)
The Jewish Museum (Židovské Muzeum), founded in 1906 after the reconstruction of Josefov, includes the collectively

Czech out the Cubism at the Black Madonna.

managed Old Jewish Cemetery (see p. 38), Ceremonial Hall, Maisel Synagogue, Pinkas Synagogue (see p. 40), Spanish Synagogue (see p. 40) and Klaus Synagogue. The separately run Old-New Synagogue (see p. 22) can be visited independently, or with the Jewish Museum. It's a fascinating grouping, but tourist prices are grossly inflated.
✉ U starého hřbitova 3a, Josefov
☎ 22 31 71 91
e www.jewishmuseum .cz Ⓜ Staroměstská ☺ Nov-Mar: Sun-Fri 9am-4pm; Apr-Oct: Sun-Fri 9am-6pm; closed Jewish holidays Ⓢ 290/ 200Kč ⓰ only Old Jewish Cemetery, Maisel & Spanish synagogues

Lapidárium (4, C8)
There are some intimidating rocks in this National Museum repository of Bohemian stone sculpture (11th-19th centuries). Foremost among them are the three Kouřim Lions (the country's oldest stone

sculpture), Jan Bendl's original equestrian statue of St Wenceslas and a number of Charles Bridge statues.
✉ Fairgrounds (Výstaviště 422), Holešovice
☎ 33 37 56 36
e www.nm.cz
Ⓜ Nádraží Holešovice, then tram 5, 12, 17, 53 or 54 to Výstaviště ☺ Tues-Fri noon-6pm, Sat-Sun 10am-6pm Ⓢ 20Kč ⓰

Lobkowicz Palace (2, B5) The Lobkovický palác contains the highly recommended National Museum exposition 'Monuments of the National Past', covering Czech history from settlement to the attempted democratic revolution of 1848. Take your time, refer to the well-written notes and look out for the old guns so clunky they look futuristic.
✉ Jiřská 3, Prague Castle, Hradčany
☎ 33 35 44 67
e www.nm.cz
Ⓜ Malostranská; Hradčanská ☺ Tues-Sun 9am-5pm Ⓢ 40/20Kč ⓰

Mucha Museum (3, G10) Learn about the man who created the distinctive Parisian Art Nouveau posters Sarah Bernhardt fell in love with, which you've seen framed in many a Prague cafe. Also shown in crisp detail are Mucha's *Slav Epic* paintings, his drawings, and some interesting photographs, including one which seems to show Gauguin, minus his pants,

Much Ado About Mucha

The Mucha Museum does a great job of presenting the life and times of Alfons Mucha, aided by the cooperation it receives from the celebrated artist's grandson and daughter-in-law in the guise of the Mucha Foundation. But greatness can be a curse, and this is highlighted in a museum blurb that describes how Mucha's mother used to tie a pencil around the then-toddler's neck so he could draw as he crawled about. Without any trace of irony, the blurb says 'Very few of his early drawings survive'.

playing the harmonium in Mucha's studio.

✉ **Panská 7, Nové Město** ☎ **628 41 62**
✉ www.mucha.cz
Ⓜ **Můstek**
🕐 10am-6pm
💲 120/60Kč ♿

Museum of the City of Prague (3, C14)

Offering a stimulating presentation of Prague from prehistory to the late 18th century, Muzeum hlavního města Prahy contains the original Astronomical Clock calendar-plate painted by Josef Mánes, and the remarkable paper model of Prague assembled by Antonín Langweil 1826-34, containing 2000 'buildings' with minute embellishments like broken windows. Also see Antonio Sacchetti's mural in the main stairwell.

✉ **Na poříčí 52, Nové Město** ☎ **24 81 67 72**
✉ www.muzeumprahy.cz Ⓜ **Florenc**
🕐 Tues-Sun 9am-6pm
💲 30/15/45Kč, 1Kč 1st Thurs of every month (museum open to 8pm)

Náprstek Museum

(3, G5) The museum is a catalogue of artefacts from non-European cultures, built around the 19th-century collection of local industrialist and wanderer Vojta Náprstek. Though items can be visually impressive, the presentation suffers from an unfortunately virulent strain of 'exotica' (a disease causing an absence of cultural context); labels are in Czech only.

✉ **Betlémské náměstí 1, Staré Město**
☎ 22 22 00 18
✉ www.aconet.cz/npm Ⓜ **Národní třída**
🕐 Tues-Sun 9am-12.15pm & 1-5.30pm
💲 40/20Kč, free 1st Fri of every month ♿

Pop Museum (2, H5)

The Muzeum a archiv populární hudby boasts a down-to-earth display of the best of Czech poppers from 1956-72. Check out Czech electric guitars, which reached their zenith with an award at the 1958 Brussels expo, and the melodies of Jiří Schelinger, Miki Volek and Plastic People of the Universe.

✉ **Besední 3, Malá Strana** ☎ 57 31 47 76
✉ www.popmuseum.cz Ⓜ **Národní třída**, then tram 22, 23 or 57 to Újezd 🕐 Fri-Sun 2-6pm (after-hours visits possible; ☎ 0603 41 91 98) 💲 30Kč

Postal Museum

(3, B10) Philatelists will get all gummy over the Muzeum Poštovní Známky and its collection of Czech and European stamps, including the famed 'Penny Black', the world's first stamp issued in 1840. Others will note the work of Czech artist Josef Navrátil.

✉ **Nové mlýny 2, Nové Město** ☎ 231 20 06
Ⓜ **Náměstí Republiky**
🕐 Tues-Sun 9am-noon & 1-5pm 💲 25/10Kč, ticket sales stop at 11.30am & 4.30pm

Smetana Museum

(3, F4) Bedřich Smetana (1824-84) is considered *the* Bohemian composer and wrote the well-known works *Dalibor a Libuše* (Dalibor & Libuše) and *Má Vlast* (My Country) – *Má Vlast* is the composition that kicks off the annual Prague Spring festival at Municipal House. This educational museum presents Smetana's life, music and possessions in great detail, including his piano circa 1860.

✉ **Novotného lávka, Staré Město** ☎ 22 22 00 82 Ⓜ **Staroměstská**
🕐 Wed-Mon 10am-noon & 12.30-5pm
💲 50Kč

GALLERIES

Convent of St Agnes
(3, B8) Upstairs in the peaceful 1231 sanctum of Klášter Sv Anežky is an excellent National Gallery exhibition of Bohemian and Central European medieval art (13th-16th centuries); particularly striking are the altarpieces from the Cistercian monastery at Vyšší Brod. The ground-floor cloister has a tactile presentation of 12 casts of medieval sculptures accompanied by Braille plaques.
✉ Anežská 1, Josefov
☎ 24 81 06 28
e www.ngprague.cz
Ⓜ Staroměstská; Náměstí Republiky
☉ Tues-Sun 10am-6pm
⑤ gallery 100/50/150Kč, gallery & churches 120/60/150Kč; free 1st Wed of every month ⚿

Convent of St George (2, B4)
This old Benedictine convent building (Klášter Sv Jiří) has an exhibition of Bohemian art from early mannerist works to baroque, featuring artists such as Karel Škréta and Jan Kupecký. More eclectic inclusions are an Ottoman tent brought to Bohemia in 1616, and a set of amputation instruments used (without anaesthesia) until 1846. Top floor has impressive statuary.
✉ Jiřské náměstí 33, Prague Castle, Hradčany ☎ 57 32 05 36
e www.ngprague.cz
Ⓜ Malostranská; Hradčanská ☉ Tues-Sun 10am-6pm ⑤ 90Kč, free 1st Wed of every month ⚿

Galerie MXM (3, G1)
Hidden in an artistically unkempt courtyard accessed through a gateway opposite Pelclova, this private gallery is devoted to showcasing the creativity of younger artists, without any sign of stylistic restrictions. There's always something interesting (if not always palatable) on show.
✉ Nosticova 6, Malá Strana ☎ 57 31 11 98
Ⓜ Národní třída, then tram 22, 23 or 57 to Újezd ☉ Tues-Sun noon-6pm ⑤ free ⚿

Gambra Surrealist Gallery (5, A2)
Tiny, fascinating haven for Czech and Slovak surrealist artists, run by Eva and Jan Šankmajer, who also display their own often vividly grotesque work. Also stocks topical Czech books and periodicals.
✉ Černínská 5, Hradčany ☎ 20 51 47 85
e home.nextra.cz/~surreal/gambra
Ⓜ Malostranská, then tram 22 or 23 to Pohořelec
☉ Mar-Oct: Wed-Sun noon-6pm; Nov-Feb: Sat-Sun noon-6pm

House at the Golden Ring (7, B7)
Much of the Renaissance Dům U zlatého prstenu is taken up by a fascinating City Gallery of Prague exhibition of 20th-century art (1900-90). Stand-outs are František Hudeček's *Golem*, Rudolf Němec's striking *Shade of Blue*, and the art-literature-stocked reading room on the 2nd floor.
✉ Týnská 6, Staré Město ☎ 24 82 70 22
e www.citygallery prague.cz Ⓜ Náměstí Republiky ☉ Tues-Sun 10am-6pm ⑤ 60/30/120Kč ⚿

House of the Stone Bell (7, B6)
This 14th-century house was subjected to a baroque face-lift before having corrective architectural surgery in the 1950s to restore its Gothic look. Its two chapels are now used by City Gallery of Prague for occasional exhibitions.
✉ Staroměstské náměstí 13, Staré Město
☎ 24 82 75 26
e www.citygallery prague.cz Ⓜ Staroměstská; Můstek
☉ Tues-Sun 10am-6pm
⑤ 60/30Kč

Something for Nothing
A healthy number of museums and galleries in Prague prescribe to the idea of public days, where entry fees are waived or reduced to a token amount. All National Gallery branches hold their open day on the first Wednesday of every month, and the National Museum and associated City of Prague museum have theirs on the first Monday and Thursday of each month respectively. Freebies are noted in the relevant reviews. Children between six and 10 years of age often gain free admittance to exhibitions and to fitness facilities.

See artistry at work in the Kinský Palace.

Kinský Palace (7, B6)
Thrusting its double-fronted rococo facade into the square is the late baroque Palác Kinských. Its balcony was used by Klement Gottwald in 1948 to proclaim communist dominance, and the National Gallery uses the palace for an exhibition of drawing and graphics from the Middle Ages to today.
✉ **Staroměstské náměstí 12, Staré Město** ☎ 24 81 07 58 **e** www.ngprague.cz **Ⓜ Staroměstská; Můstek** ⏰ **Tues-Sun 10am-6pm** ⑤ **90/40/200Kč, free 1st Wed of every month** ♿

Mánes Gallery (4, F7)
A 1930s incarnation of a gallery previously founded by artist Josef Mánes and friends in Kinský Gardens to rattle the cage of a complacent art world. Takes the notion of innovation seriously by staging everything from antique fairs to photographic exhibitions on international exodus.
✉ **Masarykovo nábřeží 250, Nové Město**
☎ 24 93 14 10
Ⓜ Karlovo Náměstí
⏰ **10am-8pm**
⑤ **60/30Kč**

Nová síň (3, J5)
Czech contemporary art and photography adorn the stark white walls of this private gallery. An example of the satisfyingly unpredictable contents was a recent exhibition called 'Atlas of the Human Embryo and Foetus', with beautiful yet disturbing images.
✉ **Voršilská 3, Nové Město** ☎ 29 20 46 **Ⓜ Národní třída** ⏰ **Tues-Sun 11am-6pm** ⑤ **free**

Sternberg Palace (5, A5) Accessed by a passageway next to Archbishop's Palace, the baroque Šternberský palác serves as a branch of the National Gallery and has a recently reinstalled collection of 'Old European Art', including works by El Greco, Rembrandt and Rubens.
✉ **Hradčanské náměstí 15, Hradčany** ☎ 20 51 45 99 **e** www.ngprague.cz **Ⓜ Malostranská**

⏰ **Tues-Sun 10am-6pm** ⑤ **90Kč, free 1st Wed of every month** ♿ **ground floor only**

Strahov Gallery (5, D2)
Billed as one of Central Europe's most important monastic collections, the exhibits in the Strahovská obrazárna run the gamut of styles from Gothic and Rudolphine to rococo and baroque. Includes 19th-century Czech, and Italian and Flemish art.
✉ **Strahovské nádvoří 1, Strahov Ⓜ Malostranská, then tram 22 or 23 to Pohořelec** ⏰ **Tues-Sun 9am-noon & 12.30-5pm** ⑤ **35/20Kč**

Summer Palace (2, A5)
The 16th-century Renaissance Královský Letohrádek has a prominently curved copper roof. Often referred to as the 'Belvedere', it was recently restored and opened to the public to host part of a wide-ranging Prague Castle exhibition.
✉ **Prague Castle, Hradčany** ☎ 24 37 33 68 **(information centre)** **e** www.hrad.cz **Ⓜ Malostranská, then 22 or 23 to Pražský hrad** ♿

U prstenu Gallery (7, F4) Mostly occupied by fresh, innovative exhibitions of local and international artists; instalments usually change monthly. There are prints and lithographs for sale, display cases filled with jewellery and other creations of Czech artisans, and a restful cafe out back.
✉ **Jilská 14, Staré Město** ☎ 24 22 28 64 **e** www.uprstenu.cz **Ⓜ Národní třída** ⏰ **11am-7pm** ⑤ **20/10Kč**

NOTABLE BUILDINGS & MONUMENTS

Dancing Building
(4, F7) The Dancing Building (Tančící dům) is a remarkably successful attempt at integrating avant-garde architecture into an old neighbourhood. Nicknamed the 'Astaire & Rogers Building' by its creators, Vlado Milunić and Frank O Gehry, its fluid, just-melted form seems inexplicably natural. Behind the topmost metal and glass is one of Prague's best restaurants, **La Perle de Prague** (see p. 76).
✉ Rašínovo nábřeží 80, Nové Město
Ⓜ Karlovo Náměstí ♿

'ague's primadonna: a ew face in an old town

Estates Theatre (7, D7)
Prague's oldest theatre is one of its most beautiful neoclassical achievements. Opening as the Nostitz Theatre in 1783, it was the venue Mozart had in mind for the premiere of *Don Giovanni*. Later renamed after the collective Bohemian nobility, the Stavovské Divadlo is now a principal Prague venue for concerts, ballets and operas.
✉ Ovocný trh 1, Staré Město ☎ 24 21 50 01,
🌐 www.narodni-divadlo.cz Ⓜ Můstek
🕐 box office (Kolowrat Palace) Mon-Fri 10am-6pm, Sat-Sun 10am-12.30pm & 3pm-6pm

František Palacký Monument (4, F7)
The best way to admire Stanislav Sucharda's bronze tribute to famed 19th-century historian Palacký, who helped lead the way during the Czech National Revival, is to stand beneath it and gaze up at the expressions on the monument's figures, particularly those behind the main man.
✉ Palackého náměstí, Nové Město Ⓜ Karlovo Náměstí ♿

Jan Hus Statue (7, C5)
Diverting pedestrian traffic in the middle of Old Town Square is the statuesque presence of Jan Hus, erected 6 July 1915 on the 500th anniversary of the reformer's execution. The

The Estates has seen a Bohemian rhapsody or two.

sombreness of Ladislav Šaloun's statue, which casts Hus alongside fighters, and a mother and child representing a reborn Czech nation, is relieved a little by encircling flower beds.
✉ Staroměstské náměstí, Staré Město
🚃 17, 18, 51, 54 to Staroměstská ♿

Klementinum (7, D2)
The massive Klementinum was a Jesuit college before becoming part of Charles University in 1773. From the inner courtyard, catch a tour of the grand baroque library – bookworms note that the pre-18th-century tomes are off-limits – and the 52m-high, recently reconstructed Astronomical Tower.
✉ Mariánské náměstí, Staré Město ☎ 0603 23 12 41 Ⓜ Staroměstská 🕐 Apr-Jun: Mon-Fri 2-8pm, Sat-Sun 10am-8pm; Jul: 10am-9pm; Aug-Oct: Mon-Fri 2-9pm, Sat-Sun 10am-9pm 💲 100/50/140Kč ♿ library only

Žižkov Hill

The TV Tower may rule the skyline of Žižkov, but it's the large pile of earth separating this old working-class suburb from neighbouring Karlín that history will favour. It was on top of this hill in 1420 that Jan Žižka, commander-in-chief of Hussite forces, led a group of 1000 in defeating a 10,000-strong army belonging to crusading Holy Roman Emperor Sigismund. One of the largest equestrian statues in the world was erected in his honour on what is now called Žižkov Hill.

Main Train Station

(3, G13) The main train station (Hlavní Nádraží) is but a shambling Art Nouveau impression of its former self. The lofty dome, stained glass, and carved faces of women symbolising 'Prague, Mother of Cities' – all on the upper level – are now witnessed only by transients grabbing a coffee in the cafe spread around the balcony.
✉ **Wilsonova, Nové Město** Ⓜ **Muzeum** ♿

Old Jewish Cemetery

(7, A3) Full of tilting sarcophagi and cascading tombstones, this nearly 600-year-old cemetery (Starý Židovský Hřbitov) is a surviving cornerstone of the Jewish community's long past, now part of the Jewish Museum. It has a rarefied, carefully preserved atmosphere (though large tour groups tend to disrupt it) and a Braille trail for the visually impaired.
✉ **Široká, Josefov**
☎ **22 31 71 91**
ⓔ **www.jewishmuseum .cz** ⊘ **Nov-Mar: Sun-Fri 9am-4pm; Apr-Oct: Sun-Fri 9am-6pm; closed Jewish holidays** ⑨ **Jewish Museum: 290/200Kč** ♿

Powder Tower

(7, C10) There are fine views from this 65m-high neo-Gothic tower (Prašná Brána), built in 1475 and used to store gunpowder in the 18th century, now with an appropriately sooty look and a photo exhibit on the Prague skyline. Watch the children on the way up, particularly while navigating the large, steep stairs up to the 1st-floor ticket office.
✉ **Na příkopě, Staré Město** Ⓜ **Náměstí Republiky** ⊘ **Apr-Oct 10am-6pm (ticket sales end 5.30pm)** ⑨ **30/20Kč**

Students Memorial

(3, H6) Under the arches at Národní 16 is a wall-plaque with the metal-frozen image of numerous hands clamouring for peace, inscribed with the date '17.11.89'. It commemorates the day students marching in remembrance of those killed during an anti-Nazi protest 50 years earlier were clubbed by police. Subsequent protests quickly saw the end of communist reign.
✉ **Národní 16, Nové Město** Ⓜ **Národní třída** ♿

TV Tower (4, E9)

This 216m tower (Televizní Věž) is the tallest thing in Prague. When a clear day graces the 'Žižkov Needle' viewing deck, you can see forever – actually up to 100km away, though to identify some of the tiny shapes below you'll need to use the telescope (10Kč/90secs). Would anyone care to explain why the tower has giant babies crawling up its exterior?
✉ **Mahlerovy sady 1, Žižkov** ☎ **67 00 57 78**
ⓔ **www.tower.cz**
Ⓜ **Jiřího Z Poděbrad**
⊘ **10am-11pm**
⑨ **120/60Kč** ♿

The moody and melancholy Jewish Cemetery

Juliet Coombe

PLACES OF WORSHIP

Basilica of St George
(2, B4) Bazilika Sv Jiří might have a baroque facade but deep down it's still a 10th-century Romanesque building, almost austere after the richness of St Vitus. There's a fantastic Otto Herbert Hajek Christ-on-a-trunk sculpture, and the chapels of St Ludmila and St John of Nepomuk are splendid. Catch one of the concerts here.
⊠ **Prague Castle, Hradčany** ☎ **24 37 33 68 (information centre)** 📧 **www.hrad.cz** Ⓜ **Malostranská; Hradčanská** ◷ **Apr-Oct 9am-5pm, Nov-Mar 9am-4pm** Ⓢ **120/60/180Kč for 3-day ticket to Castle highlights** ♿

Bethlehem Chapel
(3, G5) Betlémská Kaple is notable for its simplicity, in keeping with the Protestant reforms that dictated its construction in 1391. Jan Hus launched his campaign here, tying in with a resurgent nationalism that saw services in Czech rather than Latin; upstairs is an exhibit on Hus. The chapel was destroyed in 1786 but was authentically reconstructed 1950-52.
⊠ **Betlémské náměstí, Staré Město** Ⓜ **Národní třída** ◷ **Apr-Oct 9am-6pm, Nov-Mar 9am-5pm** Ⓢ **30Kč** ♿

Church of Our Lady of the Snows
(3, H8) It feels like it *could* snow from the frosty heights of this Gothic church (Kostel Panny Marie Sněžné). Its towering altar is the city's highest, and uses a combination of height and oversized decoration to effectively win your devotion. The church's lovely front courtyard is accessed through the archway of the Austrian Cultural Institute.
⊠ **Jungmannovo náměstí 18, Nové Město** Ⓜ **Můstek** ◷ **6.30am-7.15pm**

Church of St Francis of Assisi
(3, E4) Run by a Czech order of crusaders established in the 12th century, the Kostel sv Františka z Assisi has an interior circled by alabaster saints and a startling fresco of the *Last Judgement* by WL Reiner on the underside of its cupola. The adjacent underground chapel is weirdly decorated with Gaudi-esque stalactites, and there are regular concerts featuring the second-oldest organ in Prague.
⊠ **Křížovnické náměstí, Staré Město** ☎ **concert box office 21 10 82 66** Ⓜ **Staroměstská** ◷ **Tues-Sat 10am-1pm & 2-6pm, concerts Apr-Oct 9pm** Ⓢ **church 40/20Kč; concerts 390/350Kč**

Church of St Michael
(4, F6) Hidden in the hillside tangle of Kinský Gardens is this interesting church (kostel sv Michala), an 18th-century wooden structure brought over from a Ukrainian village piece by piece and reassembled on Petřín Hill. It's boarded up, but if you're in the area it's worth viewing; take a map or it may take you a while to find it.
⊠ **Kinský Gardens, Petřín Hill, Smíchov** Ⓜ **Anděl**

Church of the Most Sacred Heart of Our Lord
(4, F10) You can't help but be impressed by the imagination of Slovenian architect Josip Plečník, who in 1932 managed to anchor what looks like a stone freighter with a clocktower for a wheelhouse in the middle of náměstí Jiřího z

Cold comfort: Czechs find solace in the Church of Snows.

Josefov

Jews settled in Prague in the 10th century but in the 13th century were forced into a ghetto when Rome demanded separation of the Jewish and Christian populations. Also called Jewish Town, the ghetto existed until 1848, when enlightened Emperor Joseph II had its walls demolished. The new Jewish district was subsequently named Josefov after him and became an official entity of the city.

From 1893, city administrators spent two decades re-flavouring the area with Art Nouveau buildings. During WWII, the Nazis were responsible for the deaths of three-quarters of the local Jewish community and, not long afterwards, the communist regime spurred the emigration of many thousands more. It's estimated that the current Prague community numbers 5000-6000 people.

Poděbrad. The church (Kostel Nejsvětějšího Srdce Páně) is right next to the metro, though you'll probably have to shuffle through a skateboarding crowd to reach it.
⊠ náměstí Jiřího z Poděbrad 19, Vinohrady ☎ 27 38 00
Ⓜ Jiřího Z Poděbrad
☺ services Mon-Sat 8am & 6pm; Sun 7am, 9am, 11am & 6pm

Emmaus Monastery

(4, G7) Golden-horned 14th-century Benedictine monastery (Klášter Emauzy) with a Gothic church (St Mary) that bore some aggression from Allied bombs towards the end of WWII; now partly occupied by scientific organisations. At the time of research it was being accosted by work crews, hopefully for public enjoyment – though slightly derelict now, the cloister and grounds have an enigmatic atmosphere.
⊠ Vyšehradská 49, Nové Město
Ⓜ Karlovo Náměstí

Pinkas Synagogue

(7, A2) Part of the Jewish Museum (see p. 33), Pinkasova Synagóga was built in 1535 and reconstructed in the 1950s as a memorial to Jewish victims of the attempted Nazi genocide in Bohemia and Moravia. The synagogue has the sobering sight of 77,297 names marked in a context of community and family on its pale interior walls, and affecting drawings by children imprisoned in Terezín (see p. 55).
⊠ Široká 3, Josefov
☎ 22 31 71 91
ⓔ www.jewishmuseum.cz Ⓜ Staroměstská
☺ Nov-Mar: Sun-Fri 9am-4pm; Apr-Oct: Sun-Fri 9am-6pm; closed Jewish holidays
Ⓢ Jewish Museum: 290/200Kč

Rotunda of the Holy Cross

(3, H4) This 12th-century church (Kaple Sv Kříže) is significant as one of the few Romanesque structures still left standing in Prague and one of the oldest buildings in the city. Its modest style, with remnants of Gothic frescoes inside, comes as a visual relief after the soaring splendour of other local places of worship.
⊠ cnr Konviktstá & Karoliny Světlé, Staré Město Ⓜ Národní třída
☺ services Tues 6pm, Sun 5pm

The Rotunda: remnants of a fallen empire

Spanish Synagogue

(3, C7) Dating from 1868 and part of the Jewish Museum collective, this beautiful synagogue (Španělská Synagóga) has a fantastic Moorish interior swirling with gilt, polychrome and stucco motifs. There's an exhibition on Jewish history that goes back to the enlightenment, and concerts are regularly held here.
⊠ Vězeňská 1, Josefov
☎ 22 31 71 91 ⓔ office@jewishmuseum.cz; www.jewishmuseum.cz
Ⓜ Staroměstská
☺ Nov-Mar: Sun-Fri 9am-4pm; Apr-Oct: Sun-Fri 9am-6pm; closed Jewish holidays
Ⓢ Jewish Museum: 290/200Kč ♿

PARKS & GARDENS

Chotek Park (3, A2)

Landscaped in 1833, Chotkovy sady stretches east of the Summer Palace, and is Prague's oldest public park. Usually devoid of humanity, the park allows luxurious views south down the Vltava, where the river's bridges obligingly line themselves up to make it into your photo.
✉ **Chotkovy sady, Hradčany**
Ⓜ **Malostranská** &

Františkánská zahrada (3, H8)

The garden of the former Franciscan Ursuline Convent is now a tiny enclosed park. Its paved walkways and low-lying greenery are a pleasant shelter from the surrounding activity, or they would be if the air wasn't so full of city construction sounds. Mini-hedgerows unkindly keep you off the grass, and there's a diminutive play area for tots.
✉ **Jungmannovo náměstí, Nové Město**
Ⓜ **Můstek** ☼ mid-Apr

to mid-Sept: 7am-10pm; mid-Sept to mid-Oct: 7am-8pm; mid-Oct to mid-Apr: 8am-7pm &

Garden on the Ramparts (2, C4)

Apart from offering a spectacular vista, the finely manicured Zahrada Na valech lets you get close to the castle's exterior, with its sloping concrete buffers. A great place to perch on a retaining wall in the sun, though you'll find snap-happy people will clamber over you to have their photo taken with Prague as their personal backdrop.
✉ **Prague Castle, Hradčany** ☎ **24 37 33 68 (information centre)**
🅴 **www.hrad.cz**
Ⓜ **Malostranská**
☼ Apr-Oct 10am-6pm &

Letná Gardens (3, A4)

Letenské sady has giddy views of the city and river from the concrete deck around its gigantic, slightly

The Castle gardens, in an ivy league of their own

arthritic-sounding metronome. The device was built on the spot where an equally gigantic statue of Stalin was hoisted in 1955, then pulled down in 1962. Circuses occasionally set up just north of the gardens.
✉ **Letenské sady, Letná** Ⓜ **Malostranská, then tram 12 to Čechův most; Hradčanská, then tram 1, 8, 25, 26, 51 or 56 to Sparta** & approach park from northern side

Royal Garden (2, A4)

Originally planted in 1535, Královská zahrada grants a royal respite from the crowded arena of Prague Castle. Wander through groves of mature trees and past entrancing buildings like the Renaissance Ball-Game House and Summer Palace. If the fountain in front of the palace is

Enjoy the Franciscan garden – but keep off the grass!

flowing, you might get to hear why it's called the 'Singing Fountain'.

✉ Mariánské hradby, Hradčany ☎ 24 37 33 68 (information centre) ℮ www.hrad.cz Ⓜ Malostranská, then 22 or 23 to Pražský hrad ⏱ Apr-Oct 10am-6pm

Stromovka (4, B7)

The huge expanse of trees and clearings to the west of the Fairgrounds is sometimes called Royal Deer Park because of its use as a hunting preserve in the Middle Ages. Weaving between the wonderful copses are lots of walking/cycling trails.

✉ Stromovka, Bubeneč Ⓜ Nádraží Holešovice, then tram 5, 12, 17, 53, 54 to Výstaviště ♿

Vojan Park (3, D2)

Once part of a Carmelite convent, this sleepy park (Vojanovy sady) went public in 1955 under the moniker of a famous actor of the time. The old surrounding walls keep a lot of the area's noise out, but

there's a minimalist children's play area near the front entrance where you can create some. Dogs and bikes are not permitted.

✉ U lužického semináře, Malá Strana ☎ 53 67 91 Ⓜ Malostranská ⏱ 8am-7pm (to 5pm Nov-Mar) ♿

Vrtbov Garden (2, E4)

Steeply-terraced baroque garden (Vrtbovská zahrada) established 1715-20, sheltering a dozen elegant sculptures, a fountain, a passage decorated with Reiner frescos, and numerous romantic couples casually trying to avoid each other. There's also a wondrous view to the castle.

✉ Karemlitská 25, Malá Strana ☎ 57 53 14 80, 0603 233 912 ℮ www.vrtbovska.cz Ⓜ Malostranská ⏱ 10am-6pm ⑤ 20Kč

Vyšehrad Gardens (4, G7)

The small, secluded parks of ancient Vyšehrad make for an excellent escape when you need

a break from the city. Do a circuit around the ramparts to find your preferred slice of solitude, whether it's the benches on the southern side overlooking the small boat harbour, or the grassy lea near the rotunda.

✉ Soběslavova 2, Vyšehrad ☎ 24 92 07 35, 24 91 99 39 Ⓜ Vyšehrad ⏱ Apr-Oct: 9.30am-6pm; Nov-Mar: 9.30am-5pm ♿

Wallenstein Garden (3, C1)

Magnificent garden complex (Valdštejnská zahrada) built in the early 17th century with a baroque flavour borrowed from the domineering palace behind it; a perfect spot for concerts. Many of the original statues and other cultural trimmings were ransacked by the Swedes during the Thirty Years' War. It was undergoing intensive landscaping at the time of research.

✉ Letenská, Malá Strana Ⓜ Malostranská ⏱ May-Sept: 9am-7pm; Apr & Oct: 10am-6pm ♿

SQUARES & STREETS

Celetná Ulice (7, C8)

The name of this pedestrianised strip of pastel facades linking Old Town Square with náměstí Republiky derives from the word *caltnéří*, which referred to the street's 14th-century bakers of *calty* (buns). It's still occupied by commerce, but now has a cluster of upmarket jewellery, perfume and Bohemian crystal shops.

✉ Celetná ulice, Staré Město Ⓜ Náměstí Republiky ♿

Charles Square (4, F7)

Prague's biggest square (Karlovo náměstí) was created in the mid-14th century and has been coloured in with parkland greenery. New Town Hall is at its northern end, while the south is crowded by Charles University's baroque Faust House. Look east for the golden-silhouetted statues of baroque St Ignatius Church.

✉ Karlovo náměstí, Nové Město Ⓜ Karlovo Náměstí ♿

Hradčanské Náměstí (2, C1)

Prague Castle's 'front yard' is an attraction in its own right, a large paved space bordered by the architectural melange of the Archbishop's Palace and the very loud sgraffito of the Schwarzenberg Palace. The square's small park is punctured by Ferdinand Brokoff's plague column, marking the Black Death's death in 1679.

✉ Hradčanské náměstí, Hradčany Ⓜ Malostranská ♿

Jan Palach Square
(7, A1) This modest concrete-and-grass patchwork (náměstí Jana Palacha) is dedicated to philosophy student Jan Palach, who set himself ablaze on 16 January 1969 to protest the Warsaw Pact invasion of Prague. A death-mask plaque of Palach is attached to the Univerzity Karlovy faculty he attended across the road.
✉ **náměstí Jana Palacha, Josefov**
Ⓜ **Staroměstská** ♿

Loretánské Náměstí
(5, B3) This 18th-century plot was originally the forecourt for the enormous Černin Palace, current residence of the Foreign Ministry. On its eastern side is the spiritually significant Loreta (see p. 17), and quietly going about its business to the north is the oldest still-operational Capuchin Monastery in Bohemia. A quiet stumble down the heavily cobblestoned Černinská nearby is a must.
✉ **Loretánské náměstí, Hradčany** Ⓜ **Malostranská, then tram 22 or 23 to Pohořelec** ♿

Lucerna Passage (3, J9)
This is a great Art-Nouveau labyrinth under Lucerna Palace, bordered by Wenceslas Square, Štěpánská, V Jámě and Vodičkova. Apart from numerous shops, restaurants and a music club, this dimly-lit hidey-hole (Pasáž Lucerna) also has an upside-down, turned-around version of the famous Wenceslas statue dangling outside Lucerna cinema, with regards from artist David Černý.
✉ **Lucerna Passage,**

Golden Lane

Golden Lane (2, B5) is the atmospheric and usually extremely crowded little thoroughfare in the north-eastern corner of Prague Castle, which came into existence sometime after 1484, when the erection of a new outer castle wall created a passageway between itself and the older Romanesque fortifications. Originally called Zlatnická ulička (Goldsmith's Lane) after resident goldsmith guild members, it was a mini-shanty town of tiny dwellings which later evolved into 'houses' for castle artillerymen. Today, after a period when squatters ruled the roost before fanciful renovations were made, a row of 11 houses remains. They now carry out new roles as souvenir repositories.

Richard Nebesky

Nové Město
Ⓜ **Muzeum** ♿

Malé Náměstí (7, D4)
Literally a 'Little Square' but big enough for a Mary Tyler Moore twirl and hat toss. It's beautifully surrounded by baroque and neo-Renaissance facades, including the sgraffito-decorated VJ Rott building, and has a wrought-iron fountain at its centre. Can often be choked with through-traffic moving between Old Town Square and Charles Bridge.
✉ **Malé náměstí, Staré Město**
Ⓜ **Staroměstská** ♿

Malostranské Náměstí (2, D5)
Much of Malá Strana's busiest square is taken up

by a car park and the enormous perimeter of the turbo-baroque St Nicholas Church (see p. 27), with the hulking concert venue of Liechtenstein Palace (see p. 95) commanding plenty of real estate too. There are some good bars, pubs and restaurants around the square, but many more within lurching distance down side-streets.
✉ **Malostranské náměstí, Malá Strana**
Ⓜ **Malostranská** ♿

Maltézské Náměstí
(2, F5) Duck down quiet Prokopská to this attractive square, named after the Knights of Malta who established a monastery nearby. Beyond the statue of St John the Baptist is a side-street glimpse of the

Richard Nebeský

Pařížská třída: Paris meets Prague

Church of Our Lady Below the Chain. The term 'square' doesn't really do justice to the irregular shape that makes you feel there are hidden possibilities in every direction.
✉ Maltézské náměstí, Malá Strana
Ⓜ Malostranská ♿

Na Příkopě (7, D10)
Prague's High Street of upmarket goods slants down from náměstí Republiky to the northern tip of Wenceslas Square, lined with all-ages fashion and expensive essentials like fine crystal. The street continues to unveil shiny new complexes, though not always successfully: the Myslbek building (Nos 19-21), with an exterior resembling a collapsed gantry, has been widely criticised since 1996 for its impact on the streetscape.
✉ Na Příkopě, Nové Město Ⓜ Můstek; Náměstí Republiky ♿

Nerudova (2, D2)
Final steep stretch of the Royal Way running west from Malostranské náměstí, with Renaissance facades and hordes of gift shops and restaurants eyeing tourists travelling to and from the base of the castle. Significant buildings include the emblematic house of St John of Nepomuk (No 18) and the baroque Church of Our Lady of Unceasing Succour (No 24).
✉ Nerudova, Malá Strana
Ⓜ Malostranská ♿

Pařížská Třída (7, A4)
Outdoor cafes and upmarket shops mingle with some stately Art Nouveau apartment buildings on tree-lined 'Parisian Avenue', which swishes from Old Town Square north to the Vltava, where it's briefly marred by the ugly symmetry of the Inter-Continental Hotel. Well worth a self-conscious stroll, with plenty of *káva*-swilling options.
✉ Pařížská třída, Josefov
Ⓜ Staroměstská ♿

QUIRKY PRAGUE

John Lennon Wall (3, F1) From Lennon's 1980 murder until the communists' 1989 downfall, this was where activists defied the anti-pop authorities by scribbling Beatles lyrics and personal refrains. Lennonova zed got whitewashed in 1998 and now there are new odes to the bespectacled one such as 'John U are my favourite anarchist', as well as other profound graffiti like 'Mickey Mouse is Death'.
✉ Velkopřevorské náměstí, Malá Strana
Ⓜ Malostranská ♿

Museum of the Infant Jesus of Prague (2, F5)
Church dedicated to the international cult of the Infant Jesus, which began here in 1628 when Princess Lobkowitz presented a costumed wax statue of the Child Jesus to resident friars. On display in Muzeum Pražského Jezulátka are the statue's embroidered vestments and a tiny jewel-encrusted crown – just pray that Baby Gap doesn't get wind of this.
✉ Karmelitská 9, Malá Strana ☎ 57 53 36 46
e www.karmel.at/ prag-jesu
Ⓜ Malostranská
🕐 June-Sept: Mon-Sat 9.30am-9pm, Sun 1-6pm; Oct-May: Mon-Sat 9.30am-5.30pm, Sun 1-5pm ⓢ free

Muzeum Miniatur (5, C2) Anatoly Konyenko is a Siberian artist who keeps moving on to smaller and smaller things, all of them visible (kind of) in this rather strange museum. So far he's painted Ludwig van Beethoven on an apple seed, put a prayer on a human hair, and made the world's smallest book – 0.9x0.9mm, inscribed with Chekhov's *The Chameleon* in two languages.
✉ Strahovské nádvoří 10, Strahov ☎ 33 35 23 71 Ⓜ Malostranská, then tram 22 or 23 to Pohořelec 🕐 9am-5pm ⓢ 40/30/20Kč

PRAGUE FOR CHILDREN

Dětský ostrov (3, K2)
Prague's smallest island (Children's Island) is a little neglected, but there's an 'urban oasis' feel about the place that seems to attract plenty of folk pushing baby carriages. Watch the littlies, though, as there are several gaps in the surrounding fence where the Vltava is accessible.
✉ **Dětský ostrov, Prague Islands**
Ⓜ Anděl ♿

Divadlo Spejbla a Hurvínka (4, D6)
Famous theatre established in 1930 by Josef Skupa and named after his father-and-son marionette creations (Spejbl and Hurvínek respectively), which have since figured prominently in many Czech childhoods. The puppet shows range from straight comedy/drama to material with a visually 'grotesque' bent that appeals to adults too.
✉ **Dejvická 38, Dejvice**
☎ 24 31 67 84
Ⓔ www.spejbl-hur vinek.cz Ⓜ Dejvická
🕐 box office Tues-Fri 10am-2pm & 3-6pm (Wed to 7pm), Sat-Sun 1-5pm; performances Tues-Fri 10am, Sat-Sun 2pm & 4.30pm ⑤ 40Kč

Fairgrounds (4, C8)
The Fairgrounds (Výstaviště) is a sprawling enclave of pavilions, theatres and tame-but-fun amusements (particularly when one of Prague's major fairs is on), all guarded by the trade fair-hungry Palace of Industry. Theatre and concerts are held in the **Spiral Theatre** (see p. 94), **Paegas Arena** and

Theatre Pyramida (see p. 94) ; rock enthusiasts should visit the **Lapidárium** (see p. 33). The computer-conducted Křížík Fountain 'performs' to Dvořák and Queen (Ⓔ www.krizi kovafontana.cz for details).
✉ **U Výstaviště, Holešovice** ☎ 20 10 32 04, 20 10 31 11
Ⓜ **Nádraží Holešovice, then tram 5, 12, 17, 53, 54 to Výstaviště**
⑤ amusement rides 15-35Kč ♿

Maze (2, G1)
Mirror maze (Bludiště) atop Petřín Hill, where kids get to distort themselves with no lasting consequences. Apart from the funny glass, there's also an intricate diorama called 'Battle Against Swedes on Charles Bridge in 1648', set at the end of the Thirty Years' War.
✉ **Petřínské sady, Malá Strana** Ⓜ Národní třída,

then tram 22, 23 or 57 to Újezd, then funicular up hill 🕐 Apr-Aug: 10am-7pm; Sept-Oct: 10am-6pm; Nov-Mar: Sat-Sun 10am-5pm
⑤ 30/20Kč ♿

Museum of Marionette Culture (7, E1) Rooms filled with a hanging multitude of authentic, colourfully dressed marionettes from the late 17th to early 19th centuries will give the kiddies something to goggle at. Star attractions are the Czech figures Spejbl and Hurvínek (see this page). You'll find the museum (Muzeum loutkářských kultur) upstairs inside the courtyard.
✉ **Karlova 12, Staré Město** ☎ 22 22 09 28
Ⓔ www.puppetart.com
Ⓜ Staroměstská
🕐 noon-9pm
⑤ 50Kč/free

Richard Nebesky

Childhood is a wonderful time to reflect.

Kid Care

The turnover of babysitting agencies in Prague is often as high as the turnover of their charges, but a few worth contacting are: **Babysitting Service** (Elišky Krásnohorské 6, Josefov; ☎ 231 31 67, 0604 121 216), charging around 100Kč/hr for weekday care and double for weekend work; **Babysitting Praha** (☎ 0602 885 074; e www.pendulus.cz/hlidani), with 24hr care on weekends, charging from 55Kč/hr; and **Agentura Korálek** (Nad Opatovem 2140, Praha 4; ☎ 0603 513 546; e www.volny.cz/ag.koralek/), which has a big database of sitters at hand.

National Technical Museum (4, D7)

There's lots to look at and learn about in this historical warehouse of almost anything with a moving part (and some without). Národní technické muzeum includes full-to-overflowing sections on acoustics, photography, astronomy, a coal/ore mine (guided tour 45mins), and a hangar of planes, locomotive engines and vintage cars. But do restrain your child's enthusiasm around the fragile objects in the gallery.
✉ Kostelní 42, Holešovice ☎ 20 39 91 11 e www.ntm.cz
Ⓜ Hradčanská, then tram 1, 8, 25, 26, 51 or 56 to Letenské náměstí
⏰ Tues-Sun 9am-5pm
$ 70/30/150Kč, audio guide 50Kč ♿

Prague Zoo (4, A6)

How about a 10km stroll among Madagascar lemurs, jaguars, Przewalski's horses from Mongolia, kangaroos, fur seals and 500 species of rare plants? Just try and get bored at Zoo Praha.
✉ U Trojského zámku, Troja ☎ 688 18 00
e zoopraha@zoopra ha.cz Ⓜ Nádraží Holešovice, then bus 112 to Zoo Praha
⏰ Mar: 9am-5pm; Apr-May & Sept-Oct: 9am-6pm; June-Aug: 9am-7pm; Nov-Feb: 9am-4pm $ 60/30Kč ♿

Public Transit Museum (4, D5)

There's a large array of Prague's public transport icons in Muzeum městské hromadné dopravy, with bus and tram vintages from 1886 until the present day. Unfortunately you're restricted to wandering around the old vehicles rather than through them, which might test the patience of young visitors.
✉ Patočkova 4, Střešovice ☎ 33 32 24 32 Ⓜ Hradčanská, then tram 1, 8, 18, 56 or 57 to Vozovna Střešovice
⏰ Apr-Nov: Sat-Sun & public holidays 9am-5pm $ 20/8Kč ♿

Toy Museum (2, B5)

Second-biggest toy exhibition in the world (outdone only when Hugh Hefner throws a party). Muzeum hraček has playful figures from all over, including ancient Greece, but kids may quickly tire of the frozen displays. Top floor is curiously devoted to Ruth Handler's famous 1959 creation, named after her daughter Barbara.
✉ Jiřská 6, Prague Castle, Hradčany
☎ 24 37 22 94
Ⓜ Malostranská; Hradčanská
⏰ 9.30am-5.30pm
$ 40/30Kč (children 20Kč)

Virtual Game Hall (3, H8)

Sizeable and surprisingly clean games arcade where youngish folk learn how to grow up and be responsible adults like the rest of us by smashing, whacking or blasting the crap out of each other. There's Crisis Zone, Star Wars, air hockey, and virtual sports like Alpine Racer.
✉ Jungmannova 22, Nové Město ☎ 0602 318 719 Ⓜ Národní třída ⏰ 11am-11pm $ 100Kč for 70 credits (most games cost 8-11 credits)

Wax Museum (3, G8)

In an age of computer-generated actors, only the youngest kids could effectively suspend disbelief in a wax museum (Museum voskových figurín); parents will have to do it when paying the extortionate cover charge. Some figures make a decent stab at humanity, though I'd swear Pablo Picasso was really Ed Harris. Only the pallid, utterly artificial Michael Jackson looks lifelike.
✉ 28.října 13, Staré Město ☎ 24 19 52 03
e www.waxmuseum prague.cz
Ⓜ Můstek ⏰ 9am-8pm $ 120/60/250Kč

KEEPING FIT

Though Czechs have an often passionate relationship with sports, they appear to be far less devoted to fitness. Exercise for a lot of Czechs can be confined to an intensive workout of the elbow, as evidenced by their staggering consumption of beer (particularly the male of the species), or being pulled by the family yapper through one of the city's many parks. Many top-end hotels have fitness facilities like a gym and/or a small pool, sometimes open to the public as well as guests, and there are also a good number of compact private gyms. Squash courts aren't hard to find in the city centre, but tennis courts and larger pools seem to prefer the outer suburbs.

ASB Squashcentrum
(3, G9) Covertly accessed by a stairwell at the back of a car park so your all-drinking-and-smoking mates won't see you, this squash centre has a couple of decent courts, a ping-pong table, and assorted drinks and sports equipment for sale. You can cook yourself in a 'turbo' solarium from 6Kč/min.
✉ Václavské náměstí 15, Nové Město
☎ 24 23 27 52
Ⓜ Můstek ⏰ Mon-Fri 7am-11pm, Sat-Sun 8am-11pm Ⓢ squash: peak (before 9am, at lunch, after 5pm weekdays) 260-420Kč/hr; off-peak 140-260Kč/hr; concession from 99Kč/hr

Bodyisland (6, D2)
If you believe your body is an island and that your environmental policies haven't been too good lately, the staff here will help you repair the damage. Besides a gym and aerobics, you can indulge (as the local corporate crowd do) in massages, cosmetic treatment, hair-cuts and a manicure – even stress management and 'stimulation of confidence' are available.
✉ Uruguayská 6, Vinohrady

☎ 22 51 79 55
Ⓜ Náměstí Míru
⏰ Mon & Wed 8am-10pm, Tues & Thurs 7am-10pm, Fri 8am-9pm, Sat 9.30am-7.15pm, Sun 5-9pm
Ⓢ gym & aerobics 60/50Kč per hr, total body massage 350Kč/90mins

Fitcentrum Vagón
(3, H6) Downstairs in a slightly grungy arcade, this small fitness centre is stocked with the requisite gym equipment, ricochet courts (a sport similar to squash) and a solarium; massages are also offered. The centre seems particularly popular with women.
✉ Národní 25, Nové Město ☎ 21 08 55 44

Ⓜ Národní třída
⏰ Mon-Fri 7am-10pm, Sat-Sun 10am-8pm
Ⓢ single visits 45-65Kč

Fitness Club Inter-Continental (3, B6)
This place looks good, and it inspires you to look good too. The gym has lots of that metal stuff you're supposed to pick up and put down, and after a leisurely bob in the 5m jet-equipped pool you can have an espresso to really get your heart racing. Accessed from the sub-ground plaza on the river side of the hotel.
✉ náměstí Curieových 43/5, Josefov
☎ 24 88 15 25

Richard Nebeský

A stroll in the park is as strenuous as it gets for some...

e www.prague.inter
conti.com
Ⓜ Staroměstská
🕓 Mon-Fri 6am-11pm,
Sat-Sun 8am-10pm
$ 2hr sauna & pool
300/150Kč, 1hr use of
gym 180Kč, 1hr aero-
bics 180Kč

Fitness Týn (7, A7)

Friendly and professional
fitness centre, with a gym,
exercise bikes, table tennis, aerobics, a small
whirlpool (spa), and a
sauna (maximum six
people to sweat it out).
The bikes are popular and
need to be booked early.
✉ Týnská 21, Staré
Město ☎ 24 80 82 95
e www.telemedia
.cz/fittyn

Ⓜ Náměstí Republiky
🕓 Mon-Fri 7am-9pm,
Sat-Sun 10am-8pm
$ gym 85Kč/visit,
cycling machines
75Kč/1hr

Hotel Čechie (4, D11)

Čechie is really more
sports club than hotel,
with a gym, pool, tennis
and squash courts, bowl-
ing, indoor golf, football
fields, and an indoor sea
with an artificial coral reef
and a 62-berth marina
(OK, we made the last one
up, but it may as well
have that too). If you're
interested in working out
while in the city, check out
the website for the multitude of hours and prices.
✉ U Sluncové 618,

Karlín ☎ 66 19 41 11
e www.hotelcechie.cz/
e_main.htm
Ⓜ Invalidovna

Ostrov Štvanice

(3, A12) This island
north of Florenc metro has
a sporting history begin-
ning with bull, boar and
bear chases, though the
'sporting' aspect is debat-
able. More recently it has
hosted the prestigious
Štvanice tennis club and a
popular ice-skating rink.
The island is under a
development cloud with
the ice-skating all but
finished, but it's possible
the sports theme may
continue.
✉ Ostrov Štvanice,
Prague Islands
☎ tennis 24 81 78 07
Ⓜ Florenc 🕓 tennis
400-500Kč/hr **$** indoor
courts available before
9am & after 7pm; no
equipment rental

YMCA Sport
Centrum (3, D11)

Well-equipped exercise
centre where you can work
off those excess dumplings
and beerhall nights in the
sauna, pool or gym, or put
a different complexion on
things in the solarium.
Long-term passes available
for individuals and groups
(except those comprising a
construction worker, biker,
cowboy and Indian).
✉ Na poříčí 12, Nové
Město ☎ 24 87 58 11
e www.scymca.cz
Ⓜ Náměstí Republiky
🕓 Mon-Fri 6.30am-
10pm, Sat-Sun 10am-
9pm **$** single visits:
pool 1.10/0.50Kč per
min; gym 1.10Kč/min;
aerobics 65/60Kč

On Yer Bike

Cyclists have a rough time around town due to the
uneven road surface, mobile obstacles (tourists), tram
tracks and vehicle exhaust fumes. To be roadworthy,
bicycles need a bell, mudguards, all-round brakes,
front/rear pedal reflectors, a flashing tail light and a
headlight; helmets are compulsory for those under 15.
It's possible to take a bike on the metro, but only in
the last carriage, which has a limit of two bikes – if the
carriage is full or pram-occupied, you're out of luck.

Richard Nebesky

out & about

WALKING TOURS

Josefov

Josefov is Prague's Jewish district, comprising a ghetto from the 13th century until reconstruction in the late 19th century. Start at Franz Kafka's birthplace ❶, which is the same spot, but a different building. Walk north up Maiselova past the Maisel Synagogue ❷ to the Renaissance High Synagogue ❸; across the laneway is Prague's most important Jewish temple, the Old-New Synagogue ❹. Go west down U starého hřbitova alongside the Old Jewish Cemetery ❺,

SIGHTS & HIGHLIGHTS

Old-New Synagogue (p. 22)
Old Jewish Cemetery (pictured below; p. 38)
Ceremonial Hall (p. 33)
Museum of Decorative Arts (p. 19)
Jan Palach Square (p. 43)
Rudolfinum (p. 96)
Pinkas Synagogue (p. 40)
Pařížská Třída (p. 44)
Barock (p. 71)
Convent of St Agnes (p. 35)

distance 1.5km duration 1½hrs
▶ start Ⓜ Staroměstská
● end 🚊 5, 8, 14 or 53 from Revoluční, cnr Dlouhá

Richard Nebeský

Pay your respects in Josefov.

Europe's oldest. You'll pass Klaus Synagogue and Ceremonial Hall ❻, the cemetery's former mortuary, before dog-legging north to Břehová. Turn left, then left again onto 17.listopadu to reach the wonderful Museum of Decorative Arts ❼. Cross the road to Jan Palach Square ❽, and stare down the massive Rudolfinum ❾. Recross 17.listopadu and go east along Široká to Pinkas Synagogue ❿, a memorial to Jews who died during WWII. Continue east and turn left on trendy Pařížská ⓫ to grab a drink at Barock ⓬. Just north of here, turn right on Bílkova and follow it through Josefov's engaging back-streets to Kozí. Go left, then right on U milosrdných, and left up Anežská to the medieval art collection in the Convent of St Agnes ⓭.

Royal Way

The Royal Way is the ancient coronation route to Prague Castle. Start from náměstí Republiky. First leisurely drop your jaw at the Art-Nouveau splendour of Municipal House ❶, then stroll under the Powder Tower ❷ and onto Celetná ❸. Admire the cubist House of the Black Madonna ❹ before doubling back up Celetná and swinging north up Králodvorská, past the I-can-do-Art-Nouveau-too Hotel Paříž ❺ to Kotva. Turn left into Jakubská and walk down to St James Church ❻, then cross Malá Štupartská and duck into Týn Court for a pick-me-up at Ebel Coffee House ❼. Walk out of the court's western end and go past the northern door of Týn Church ❽ into Old Town Square (Staroměstské náměstí). Veer south-west

to emerge into pastel-lined Malé Náměstí ❾. Bear left, then right into Karlova. Follow Karlova through the tourist chicane and along the hulking Klementinum ❿ to Křižovnicka and Charles Bridge ⓫. Cross the Vltava and head up Mostecká into the bustle of Malostranské náměstí ⓬, where you'll greet St Nicholas ⓭ with a polite nod. Cross to the square's northern side and turn left into Nerudova ⓮, the steep road leading to the castle, cluttered with shops. Ease up the hill past beer halls and tearooms until reaching the driveway of your ultimate destination, Prague Castle ⓯.

distance 3.5km **duration** 1½hrs-2hrs
▶ **start** Ⓜ Náměstí Republiky
● **end** Ⓜ Malostranská; 🚊 12, 22, 23 or 57 from Malostranské náměstí

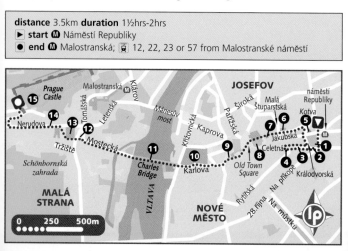

Vltava & Petřín Hill

Take your mark at Malostranská metro station. Head south down Klárov and turn right into Letenská for the manicured botany of Wallenstein Garden ❶. Back-track to Klárov and turn right down U lužického semináře. Poke your head into the sheltered confines of Vojan Park ❷ before continuing south to cross the small bridge under Charles Bridge. On your way, take a photo of the waterwheel ❸. Straight ahead is Na Kampě, where you take one of the small lanes to the right and cross the canal into Velkopřevorské náměstí, home of the John Lennon Wall ❹. Return to Na Kampě and continue south to Rybářský klub ❺, where you can eat delicious fish-food. Further south, turn right on Říční. Go to the end, turn right on Újezd, then left on U lanové dráhy to either walk or catch the funicular ❻ to the top of Petřín Hill ❼. On the hilltop, veer right along the Hunger Wall to climb Petřín Tower and groom yourself in the mirrors of the Maze ❽. Head north through the gardens to the impressive surrounds of Strahov Monastery ❾, and finish your walk with a glass of Czech wine at Oživlé Dřevo ❿.

SIGHTS & HIGHLIGHTS

Wallenstein Garden (p. 42)
Vojan Park (p. 42)
John Lennon Wall (p. 44)
Rybářský klub (p. 73)
funicular (p. 110)
Petřín Hill (p. 25)
Maze (p. 45)
Strahov Monastery (p. 28)
Oživlé Dřevo (p. 70)

Meet and greet the monks at the Strahov.

Richard Nebeský

---

distance 2.15km **duration** 2hrs
▶ **start** Ⓜ Malostranská
● **end** 🚊 22 or 23 from Keplerova, cnr Pohořelec

Wenceslas Square to Old Town Square

Begin on the National Museum steps ❶, from where you can see the entirety of Wenceslas Square before you. Cross the road to Josef Myslbek's statue of St

Wenceslas ❷, erected in 1912, and then walk down the square's western side to one of several entrances to the atmospheric Lucerna Passage ❸. Further north is the Melantrich Building ❹ – President Havel announced communism's end from its balcony in 1989. Cross the square to the impressive facade of Hotel Europa ❺, then continue north through the consumer chaos to the intersection rather hopefully called

Start bright and early at the Museum.

Richard Nebeský

distance 1.5km **duration** 1hr
▶ **start** Ⓜ Muzeum
● **end** Ⓜ Staroměstská

the 'Golden Cross' ❻. To your right is the flashy shopping strip of Na příkopě ❼, but head left through the small arcade to Jungmannovo náměstí and the entrance to the lofty Church of Our Lady of the Snows ❽. Double back and then head north up crowded Na mustků to check out Havelská Market ❾. Further north on Melantrichova is the vegetarian Country Life ❿, great for a healthy, revitalising meal before taking the final plunge into Old Town Square ⓫. You'll probably have to flail through a crowd in front of the Astronomical Clock ⓬ to get to the square's centrepiece, Jan Hus Statue ⓭.

EXCURSIONS

Karlštejn   (1, D1)

Karlštejn Castle's foundations were laid in 1348 by King/Emperor Charles IV, who felt he could no longer safely hide the crown jewels under the royal doona and needed larger fortifications for them. The result was this crag-top edifice, given a fresh medieval shape a century ago and now stormed by foreign armies of rubberneckers most days; it's the most popular and best-preserved castle in the Czech Republic. Standard tours visit internal features like the Hall of Forebears (filled with stuffy royal portraits), and the empty but interesting Audience Hall and Imperial Bedroom, but it's the view from the outside that's most impressive. Try to take a walk through the surrounding woods.

Průhonice   (1, C3)

On the southern outskirts of Prague is the small village of Průhonice, with an architecturally paranoid chateau that began as a 12th-century Romanesque settlement and then received Gothic, Renaissance and Empire shock-treatments until finally being cured with Czech neo-Renaissance therapy in the late 19th century. But the main reason for coming out here is the glorious **250ha park**, established in 1885 by Count Ernst Emanuel Silva-Tarouca and now run by the state. It's a wonderful place to simply wander around, naturally inundated with forest, meadows, small lakes, and wooded hill-crests with long rambling views. Pack a picnic lunch and come out on a weekday when the seclusion is dizzying.

INFORMATION

25km south-west of Prague
- Ⓜ Smíchovské Nádraží, then local train (35mins; 44Kč return) to Karlštejn, then a 20-25min walk to the castle through town
- ☎ 02-74 00 81 54
- ⓔ reservace@spusc.cz
- ⓘ ticket office in main courtyard
- ⏲ Apr & Oct: Tues-Sun 9am-4pm; May-June & Sept: Tues-Sun 9am-5pm; Jul & Aug: Tues-Sun 9am-6pm; Nov-Mar: Tues-Sun 9am-3pm (closed day after public holidays)
- Ⓢ 50min tour Route 1 200/100Kč, Route 2 (Chapel of the Holy Cross) 600/200Kč (this route must be booked in advance by phone)

Hit the well-trodden trail to Karlštejn.

Richard Nebeský

INFORMATION

10km south-east of Prague
- Ⓜ Opatov, then bus (15mins) No 324, 325, 328, 363 or 385 from CSAD stand (up escalator to the right as you emerge from metro)
- ☎ 02-71 01 51 11
- ⓘ park plan available from kiosk at entrance (5Kč)
- ⏲ Apr-Oct: 7am-7pm; Nov-Mar: 8am-5pm
- Ⓢ 20/10Kč

Kutná Hora (1, D5)

Kutná Hora grew from a silver-ore find in the late 13th century and soon acquired the prestige of being home to the Royal Mint and the king's residence, making it the most important place in Bohemia and one of Europe's power centres. All that changed when the silver ran out several centuries later, and Kutná Hora's decline was only compounded by the Thirty Years' War. Nowadays it's a mixture of often-striking streets, churches and assorted facades which contributed to it being World Heritage Listed by Unesco in 1996, and the slow pace and low-cost facilities of a small town.

The settlement has a nice pastel-painted central square, Palackého náměstí, where the tourist infrastructure congregates. You'll find the information centre, taxis and cafes here. To the south-west are the magnificent Gothic spires of **St Barbara's Church** (Chrám sv Barbory), begun in 1380 but only finished in the late 19th century; set aside time to simply stare up at the decorative ceiling and to peruse the lovely surrounding hillsides.

North-east of the centre, in the suburb of Sedlec, is the gruesomely fascinating handiwork of the ossuary in the **Chapel of All Saints**. The chapel became a skeletal repository in the 14th century, after plague overburdened the adjacent cemetery. František Rint, a Czech woodcarver, was responsible for arranging the myriad bones in their current stylised formations, which include crosses, chalices, a coat of arms, and a chandelier made of every bone in the human body. Local buses or taxis cover the 2km from the main square to Sedlec.

A motionless Masaryk holds court.

Richard Nebeský

Terezín   (1, A1)

The massive structure of Terezín, which includes 4km of walls and moats, was built in 1780 by Emperor Joseph II as defensive ramparts against Prussian aggression, and was subsequently used as a garrison post and then a prisoner-of-war camp during WWI. In 1940, the Lesser Fortress became a Gestapo prison, and by the end of 1941 the Main Fortress had been turned into a Nazi transit camp that eventually saw the passage of over 150,000 Jews as they were being transported to extermination camps. At the peak of its use for this horrific purpose, Terezín held 60,000 people in a space originally meant for 5000; 35,000 Jews imprisoned here died from disease, starvation or suicide.

Inside the monumental Main Fortress, on Komenského, is the **Museum of the Ghetto**, which documents the development of Nazism and the way Jewish people tried to conduct their lives in Terezín via videos, photographs, personal letters and artwork; pictures drawn by some of the many children incarcerated in Terezín are also on display at the Pinkas Synagogue (see p. 40) in Prague. There's a second branch of this museum at the corner of Tyršova and Vodárenská in the former **Magdeburg Barracks**, while 100m south of the fortress walls is the **Crematorium**, located in the Jewish cemetery. To the east of the Main Fortress is the **Lesser Fortress**, a challenging place to visit with its chilling remnants of barracks, cells and morgues. You can see it via a self-guided tour.

INFORMATION

50km north-west of Prague

Ⓜ Florenc, then bus from Florenc bus station

🖥 www.pruvodce.com/terezin/index_en.php3

ⓘ information centre in town hall, náměstí Československé armády; ☎ 0416-78 26 16, 78 22 25

🕐 Museum of the Ghetto & Magdeburg Barracks: Apr-Sept 9am-6pm, Oct-Mar 9am-5.30pm; Crematorium: Apr-Nov Sun-Fri 10am-5pm; Lesser Fortress: Apr-Sept 8am-6pm, Oct-Mar 8am-4.30pm

Ⓢ combined ticket to museum/barracks, crematorium & Lesser Fortress 150/110Kč; individual sites 130/100Kč

Richard Nebeský

Terezín's Lesser Fortress was no less brutal.

ORGANISED TOURS

If you've had enough of organising yourself for one day, let someone else do it for you. There are many companies in Prague offering tours of the city using every imaginable form of transport, including your own feet, though there's not a lot of difference between the tours offered by the larger operators.

Best Tour (3, H9)
Coach/walking tours of Prague sites, with free hotel pick-up or departure from its outlet in the Meran Hotel, Václavské náměstí 27. Decide for yourself if they live up to their name.
⊠ **U Uranie 17, Praha 7**
☎ **878 947, 0602 322 603** ⏱ **2hr tour 10.20am, 2pm & 4pm; 3.5hr tour 10.20am & 2pm** ⑤ **2hr tour 350/310/180Kč, 3.5hr tour 530/480/260Kč**

City Bike (7, B9)
Offers en-masse pedal-power tours of the city on mountain bikes. Also rents out bikes minus the tour in 2/4/6/9hr blocks – all requisite equipment like helmets and locks provided.
⊠ **Králodvorská 5, Staré Město** ☎ **0776 180 284** ⓔ **citybike@ pragueonline.cz; www.citybike.cz**
⏱ **shop 9am-7pm; 2hr rides 10am, 2pm & sunset** ⑤ **2/4/6/9hr hire 450/500/600/700Kč**

Evropská vodní doprava
(3, B6) EVD has four boats chugging various routes on the Vltava. Go for the basic 1-2hr cruises to spots between Čechův most and Vyšehrady; try to avoid the overpriced food/music tours.
⊠ **pier under Čechův most, Josefov**
☎ **24 81 00 30**
ⓔ **evd@mbox .vol.cz;**

www.evd.cz ⏱ **1hr cruise: on the hour 10am-6pm; 2hr cruise: 3pm** ⑤ **1hr cruise 200/100Kč; 2hr cruise 350/250Kč**

Oldtimer 'History Trip' (7, D4)
Take a history-slanted spin on the cobbled streets in either a vintage Praga Piccola or a just-as-vintage Praga Alfa; don't forget your straw boater and bring a parasol to twirl casually at onlookers.
⊠ **cars stationed at various locations**
☎ **0602 875 585, 0602 261 629** ⓔ **www.histo rytrip.cz** ⏱ **depart when commissioned** ⑤ **1hr tour: 1100Kč 3-person car, 1400Kč 4/5-person car**

Pragotur (7, C5)
At the Pragotur desk in the PIS you can organise private guides to do tours tailored to architecture, art and general history. However, bookings must be made in person at least two hours prior to preferred departure time, and it's expensive.
⊠ **Old Town Hall, Staroměstské náměstí**
⏱ **Mon-Fri 9am-6pm, Sat-Sun 9am-4pm** ⑤ **3hr tours for 2/3 people 1200/1500Kč**

Prague Sightseeing Tours (3, B12)
See Prague's must-sees by bus, boat or on foot. The extensive 3½hr 'grand'

coach/walking tour departs twice daily over summer. All tours can also be booked through the Čedok travel agency (18 Na příkopě; 7, E9; ☎ 24 19 71 11).
⊠ **Klimentská 52, Nové Město** ☎ **22 31 46 61**
ⓔ **pst@mbox.vol.cz; www.pstours.cz** ⏱ **vary** ⑤ **3hr walking tour 320Kč, 3.5hr bus/walking tour 590/490Kč**

Precious Legacy Tours (7, A3)
The steep rent-a-guide price will be justified if you're keen to organise a private, 'discerning' tour of Josefov with extra trimmings. If you're just after an informative tour of the museum, stick with the guides at Maisel Synagogue.
⊠ **Maiselova 16, Josefov** ☎ **232 03 98**
ⓔ **legacy_tours@ oasanet.cz; www.lega cytours.cz** ⑤ **from US$30/hr walking tours with private guide**

Vintage Tram (2, D5)
A circa-1932 tram navigates a special sightseeing run called nostalgic tram route No 91. Trips start in Malostranské náměstí and wind their way past Wenceslas Square, up to the Fairgrounds and back.
⊠ **Malostranské náměstí, Malá Strana**
☎ **96 12 49 02** ⏱ **Apr to mid-Nov 1-8pm on the hour** ⑤ **20/10Kč**

shopping

A growing entrepreneurial spirit is delivering some unique Czech commodities into Prague's marketplace. Beautiful standards such as Bohemian crystal, Czech garnets and traditional ceramics are mixing it with some inspired home-grown fashions, music, decorative glassware and wines. With the array of often excellent locally produced goods swelling by the month, why return home clutching only a bottle of your favourite aftershave or perfume?

Shopping Areas

The centre's single biggest retail zone (or perhaps zoo) is **Wenceslas Square** (3, G8), with the perimeter crammed purse-to-wallet with browsing visitors, and Czechs making beelines for their favourite stores. You can find pretty much everything here, from high fashion and music megastores to run-of-the-mill department stores and dubious souvenir hawkers. Many great places are hidden in side-alleys such as **Lucerna Passage** (3, H9).

The other main shopping drag is the extended thoroughfare comprising **Národní třída** (3, H4), **28.října** (3, G8) and **Na příkopě** (3, E9). If these were siblings, Na příkopě would be the success-riddled young gun, surrounded by expensive brand-name clothes, simply the best crystal and personal accessories, and fashionably unreadable literature. 28.října would be the confused middle child, dressing to suit the mainstream but going grungy when the mood suits. Národní třída would be the mature professional, obsessed with classy *objet d'art* glassware and exotic furniture.

Opening Hours

Local businesses usually open weekdays from 8-10am and close 5-7pm; on the weekend, count on Saturday hours being at least 10am-2pm and on many places being closed Sunday. That said, hours vary a lot: smaller outlets prefer later starts and earlier finishes to the bigger places; shops operate for an hour or two more during warmer months; and businesses in central Prague generally keep longer hours than their suburban counterparts.

Department stores tend to be open weekdays from 9am-8pm, and weekends from 10am-6pm.

Streets ahead: it takes lots of brass and class to fit in on Na příkopě.

DEPARTMENT STORES

Bílá Labut' (3, C12)
Externally looks like a derelict warehouse, internally a random layout of departments (why else would Auto Accessories be next to Lingerie?). One floor's worth of generic Euro-brand clothes, lots of shoes and travel goods, and a large toys area – parents: beware the kid-snagging Pokemon counter inside the front entrance. A sibling store is at the corner of Wenceslas Square and Wilsonova.
✉ **Na poříčí 23, Nové Město** ☎ **24 81 13 64**
Ⓜ **Náměstí Republiky**
🕐 Mon-Fri 9am-8pm, Sat 9am-6pm, Sun 10am-6pm

Dům Hudebních Nástrojů (3, G8)
Five-level amalgamation of musical instrument shops. From the basement up, there's Guitarpark and its racks of acoustic instruments and electric axes (musician's noticeboard out front), Kliment (wind instruments and sheet music), Yamamusic (keyboards, guitars, brass), Petrof (pianos), and Yamaha Classic Salon (very grand pianos).
✉ **Jungmannovo náměstí 17, Nové Město** Ⓜ **Můstek**
🕐 vary per shop

Dům Značkové Módy (3, J10) DZM stocks all the essentials of modern-day life: a perfumery with the scents of Jean Paul Gaultier, Elizabeth Arden and DKNY; gent's clothes and accessories by Carl Gross, Pierre Cardin and Marvellis; sleek womenswear from Tuzzi, Brax and Yomanis; and a floor-full of quality lingerie.
✉ **Vaclavské náměstí 58, Nové Město**
Ⓜ **Muzeum**
🕐 9am-9pm

Kotva (7, A10)
Brooding hulk of a place with five floors of stuff to convince yourself you need, from bargain-basement clothes and baby-wear down below to electronics, sports equipment and furniture upstairs. The fashion gets pricier as you climb, and you'll find the tax-free service on the ground floor.
✉ **náměstí Republiky 8** ☎ **24 80 11 11**
Ⓜ **Náměstí Republiky**
🕐 Mon-Fri 9am-8pm, Sat 9am-6pm, Sun 10am-6pm

Krone (3, H9)
Krone has that patent Prague department store I'm-in-need-of-a-good-scrub aesthetic. Standard fare here includes a basement supermarket, clothes for your entire brood, and basic white goods. Bemusing fare includes the booth on the 2nd floor selling nothing but knives and swords.
✉ **Vaclavské náměstí 21, Nové Město** ☎ **24 23 04 77** Ⓜ **Můstek**
🕐 Mon-Fri 9am-8pm, Sat 9am-7pm, Sun 10am-6pm

Tesco (3, H6)
This is a frenetic, multi-storey maze of consumerism. Highlights include baby goods on the 1st floor, luggage and sports equipment on the 2nd, an electrical department on the 4th, and the people queuing up to buy tiny, inedible pastries from a vendor by the Národní třída entrance. The basement supermarket (see p. 67) is not for the mild-mannered.
✉ **Národní 26, Nové Město** ☎ **22 00 31 11**
Ⓜ **Národní třída**
🕐 Mon-Fri 8am-9pm, Sat 9am-8pm, Sun 10am-7pm

Brace yourselves! Tesco is not for the faint-hearted.

CLOTHING & ACCESSORIES

Colette Butik (6, E1)
Womenswear from suits to gowns crafted by Czech hands for the fashionably casual, including stuff to toss nonchalantly over a shoulder or around a neck.
✉ **Koubkova 17, Vinohrady ☎ 22 52 12 01 Ⓜ Náměstí Míru** ☺ Mon-Fri 9.30am-7pm, Sat 9.30am-noon

Estuary (3, C9)
Striking a glamorous feminine pose in the confines of pasáž u Divadla v Dlouhé are in-style seasonal collections, luxurious nightwear, sharp coats and funky accessories courtesy of prominent designer Lenka K.
✉ **Dlouhá 39, Josefov ☎ 24 82 68 29 Ⓜ Náměstí Republiky** ☺ Mon-Sat 10am-6pm

Galerie Módy (3, H9)
Transform your sartorial self via a large range of contemporary clothing and must-have accessories (mostly jewellery and handbags) from Czech designers. Recent offerings in this Helena Fejková-managed emporium have included original linen jeans for both men and women.
✉ **Lucerna Passage, Štěpánská 61, Nové Město ☎ 24 21 15 14 Ⓜ Muzeum** ☺ Mon-Fri 10am-7pm, Sat 10am-3pm

Hugo Boss (3, H8)
Clothes maketh the man and unmaketh the credit card at Hugo Boss, where applying a chisel to your jaw may be your only chance of convincing one of their monumentally suave

Taxing Times

As a foreigner, it's possible to rid yourself of up to 17% value-added tax (VAT) on certain upmarket commodities by doing the following:

Buy goods worth at least 1000Kč from a shop displaying a 'Tax Free Shopping' sign; when forking out your hard-spent cash/plastic, ask for a tax-free shopping cheque (to be filled out with your name and address); get the cheque stamped by Czech customs no later than 30 days from date of purchase; finally, head for one of the payment points listed on the ubiquitous *Where to Shop Tax Free – Prague* brochures within six weeks of purchase and get your refund.

suits to let you wear it.
✉ **Jungmannovo náměstí 18, Nové Město ☎ 24 22 21 44 Ⓜ Můstek** ☺ Mon-Fri 10am-7pm, Sat 11am-6pm, Sun 1-6pm

Jackpot & Cottonfield (7, F8)
Danish style at upmarket Czech prices. Cottonfield is for the menfolk, with the usual array of cords, knits and checked shirts that are unfashionable until sold in a fashion store. Jackpot is for the womenfolk, with an assortment of florid styles designed with bohemian-wannabes in mind.
✉ **Na příkopě 13, Nové Město ☎ 24 21 37 44 Ⓜ Můstek** ☺ 10am-7pm

Karpet (2, D3)
The ground floor of the former abode of St John of Nepomuk, the Czech patron saint, is now occupied by the outlet of a Czech millinery. Karpet can cover your rug with Roaring Twenties leopard-print creations, berets, assertive Elliot Ness hats,

and chapeaux in many other styles.
✉ **Nerudova 18, Malá Strana Ⓜ Malostranská** ☺ 10am-6pm

Original Moda (3, J7)
Piece together a unique outfit at this friendly boutique that harnesses the creative services of over 15 Czech artists, all contributing small collections of unique, hand-made women's clothing and accessories – winter style is usually classical, summer's more avant-garde. Also has ceramics, and household linen in traditional Czech blueprint designs.
✉ **Jungmannova 13, Nové Město ☎ 96 24 50 33 Ⓜ Národní třída** ☺ Mon-Fri 10am-6pm, Sat 10am-1pm

Šatna (3, G5)
Prefer pre-loved to unloved? Šatna (Cloakroom) is a secondhand clothes outlet not much bigger than a changing room, where the young and wardrobe-hungry rifle through racks of Levi's, sportswear and clubbing outfits. Jeans are around

Richard Nebeský

A Lenka K design, for those chilly Prague mornings

350Kč, and leather jackets for around 1000Kč.
✉ Konviktská 13,

Staré Město Ⓜ Národní třída ⏰ Mon-Fri 11am-7pm, Sat 11am-6pm

Senior Bazar (3, F12)
Some of the gloss has rubbed off this opportunity shop since it was voted best clothes shop in the city in 1999 by trend-setting readers of the *Prague Post*, but there's still a bargain or 20 to be found in its racks. Where else could you create a fashionably mismatched suit for only 300Kč?
✉ Senovážné náměstí 18, Nové Město
☎ 24 23 50 68
Ⓜ Náměstí Republiky

⏰ Mon-Thurs 8.30am-4pm, Fri 8.30am-2pm

Siluet (3, C6)
One of two Siluet stores in Prague (second outlet is at Na Poříčí) showcasing the designs of Eva Plzáková, who has spent the past decade sharing her fashion sense – stylish look-at-me formal wear and accessories like scarves and gloves – with female clientele in the Czech capital.
✉ Široká 15, Josefov
☎ 0605 758 512
Ⓜ Staroměstská
⏰ Mon-Fri 10am-8pm, Sat-Sun 11am-6pm

JEWELLERY

Fabergé (7, A4)
So mesmerising and alluring are the contents of this richly stocked boutique that you may just find yourself dreamily wafting inside and handing over 70,000Kč for one of their sublime rings or Easter egg pendants, or 135,000Kč for a pair of illustrious cufflinks.
✉ Pařížská 15, Josefov
☎ 232 36 39 Ⓜ Staroměstská ⏰ 10am-8pm

Granát Turnov (3, C8)
Reputedly the biggest creator of Bohemian garnet-

based jewellery, Granát Turnov offers silver or gold designs ranging from the simple to the arabesque – the common factor is that they're all crammed with garnets. Granát also sells regulation pearls and diamonds, and less expensive ornaments comprising the dark-green, semi-precious stone *vltavín*.
✉ Dlouhá 30, Josefov
☎ 22 31 56 12
Ⓜ Náměstí Republiky
⏰ Mon-Fri 10am-5pm, Sat 10am-1pm

Jewellery Ametyst (3, D6) Specialises in the enigmatic Czech garnet, available in myriad jewellery settings. Also has display cases full of conspicuously chunky amber bracelets and necklaces, and other attractively combined semi-precious stones and metals. Look for the sign out front reading 'Český Granát'.
✉ Maiselova 3, Josefov ☎ 232 35 89
Ⓜ Staroměstská
⏰ 10am-7pm

Konvikt Jewellery (3, G5) Elegant and innovative jewellery, from handmade Norwegian silver pieces to variations on the garnet and amber themes. Beautiful ceramics fill out other corners of the room.
✉ Konviktská 24, Staré Město ☎ 24 23 19 20 Ⓜ Národní třída ⏰ Mon-Fri 9.30am-2pm & 2.30-6.30pm, Sat-Sun 11am-5pm

Garnet Therapy

The blood-red rock that you'll see dangling off the wrists, necks, ears and the odd eyebrow of the city's human traffic is more than likely one of the more colourful versions of the Czech garnet *(český granát)*, a popular urban accessory and an even more popular tourist purchase. Garnets aren't always red – some even lack colour – but according to traditional rumours (often embellished by retailers) the gemstone consistently wields its mystical powers to replace sadness with joy.

ARTS & CRAFTS

Art Décoratif (7, B10)
Beautiful shop dealing in Czech-made reproductions of fine Art Nouveau (mainly 1918-19) and Art Deco pieces, including lamps, prints and jewellery. It's also an outlet for the gorgeously delicate glassware created by Jarmila Plockova, grand-daughter of Alfons Mucha, who has used elements of his paintings in her work.
✉ **U Obecního domu, Staré Město** ☎ **22 00 23 50** Ⓜ **Náměstí Republiky** ☺ **10am-8pm**

Arzenal (7, B2)
Showcase for the eye-catching modern designs of Bořek Šípek, whose vivacious domestic creations – furniture, light fittings, crockery and glassware, at turns intricate and functional – are also displayed in the on-site restaurant, **Siam-I-San** (see p. 81). Some of Šípek's pieces are now in museums. Also sells the ethereal women's fashion of Japanese designer Yoshiki Hishinuma.
✉ **Valentinská 11, Staré Město** ☎ **24 81 40 99** Ⓜ **Staroměstská** ☺ **10am-midnight**

Celetná Crystal (7, C7) Not the place to visit if you're sensitive to sparkle, with a dazzling range of traditional and modern cut crystal expensively littering its three floors, accompanied by other potential gifts or souvenirs like Bohemian porcelain and garnet jewellery. If you know someone who has everything, head to the

top floor and pick out a chandelier they might like to swing from.
✉ **Celetná 15, Staré Město** ☎ **24 81 13 76** Ⓜ **Náměstí Republiky** ☺ **Apr-Oct 10am-8pm, Nov-Mar 10am-7pm**

Czech Traditional Handicrafts (7, E5)
Sizeable gallery of Czech-made handicrafts, including glycerine soap (wrap a nostril around the apple/cinnamon version), wooden toys for the kids, ceramics, linen so brightly coloured it makes your eyes water, wire-craft, pattern-stamped gingerbread, and some fine examples of *kraslice* (Easter eggs), many of which carry batik decorations.
✉ **Melantrichova 17, Staré Město** ☎ **21 63 24 99** Ⓜ **Můstek** ☺ **10am-7.30pm**

Galerie Pyramida (3, H5) Commercial gallery with many wonderfully innovative samples of artwork, statuary and decorative glass from contemporary Czech artists on display. Surrealism and grotesquery is not

uncommon – some pieces look like they've arrived direct from an auction of *A Clockwork Orange* set pieces.
✉ **Národní 11, Nové Město** ☎ **24 21 31 17** Ⓜ **Národní třída** ☺ **10am-7pm**

Galerie SoHo (3, C12)
The owners wisely decided to go with the NY moniker rather than a local contraction of 'south of Souken-ická'. Indeed, there's really nothing so-so about the top-quality commercial exhibitions of Czech glass, sculpture and graphics staged afresh here every three months. Guest artists have included Jaroslav Svoboda, who runs his own glassworks in Karlov.
✉ **Zlatnická 4, Nové Město** ☎ **232 90 91** Ⓜ **Náměstí Republiky** ☺ **Mon-Fri 10am-6pm**

Moser (7, E8)
The neo-Renaissance-style House of the Black Rose is home to an outlet of esteemed glassmaker Moser, an enterprise founded in Karlovy Vary in 1857 and famous for the

Moser adds a touch of glass.

Richard Nebesky

The quality of Bohemian glass is crystal clear.

Richard Nebeský

technical and artistic qualities of its work. On display are some extraordinary bowls, glasses and decorative glasswork, meticulously engraved and sporting Moser's characteristically deep, rich colours.

✉ **Na příkopě 12, Nové Město** ☎ **24 21 12 93** Ⓜ **Můstek**
🕐 **Mon-Fri 9am-8pm, Sat-Sun 10am-6pm**

Regena (7, E4)

In the pristine retail environment of Palace U Kočků are three floors of expensive Bohemian crystal, porcelain and other wares resulting from the creative toil of around 60 Czech craft establishments. There's also a basement gallery of glassworks, and check out the workshop on the ground

floor to see glassmakers playing with fire.
✉ **Karlova 44, Staré Město** ☎ **24 22 05 60** Ⓜ **Můstek, Staroměstská** 🕐 **10am-8pm**

Rott Crystal (7, D4)

Rott's fabulous sgraffito-covered 'shopfront' depicts tools and artisans from the days when it was a steel company. Today, it houses innumerable pieces of garnet jewellery, china and glasswork. But Rott is known best for its stock of local and imported crystal: typically exquisite examples of traditional and modern Bohemian glitter away on the upper floors.
✉ **Malé náměstí 3, Staré Město** ☎ **24 22 95 29** Ⓜ **Staroměstská** 🕐 **Apr-Oct 10am-8pm, Nov-Mar 10am-7pm**

ANTIQUES & BRIC-A-BRAC

Alma (7, B2)

Alma specialises in Art Deco and pre-1915 Art Nouveau, and also has a selection of other bits and pieces made between 1880 and 1938. Score an old Bohemian folk dancing costume, a cuckoo clock, one of the glorious Art Nouveau tea sets, or perhaps an antique doll or marionette.
✉ **Valentinská 7, Staré Město** ☎ **232 58 65** Ⓜ **Staroměstská** 🕐 **10am-6pm**

Antikvariát Karel Křenek (7, C10)

Stocks maps, prints and books created between the 16th and 19th centuries, along with folders of old photos and lithographs,

and some modern graphics. Definitely a case of the more you look, the more you'll see – some fascinating images and representations of early Prague, Bohemia and Europe are just waiting to reveal themselves.
✉ **Celetná 31, Staré Město** ☎ **231 47 34** Ⓜ **Náměstí Republiky** 🕐 **Mon-Fri 10am-6pm, Sat 10am-2pm**

Antiqua (7, F9)

This would be Dr Who's favourite store (if not for the fact that he's a fictional character) as it specialises in timepieces. Carries restored and sometimes startlingly ornate clocks and pocket-watches, and sells a small selection of paintings,

crockery and newly buffed antique bureaux.
✉ **Panská 1, Nové Město** ☎ **22 24 58 36** Ⓜ **Můstek** 🕐 **Mon-Fri 10am-6pm, Sat 10am-2pm**

Antique Art Gallery

(3, D6) Captivating array of restored antiques, with plenty of jewellery, formal accessories such as engraved compacts and cigarette boxes, and reframed paintings. Also on display are cabinets filled with grand old timepieces, porcelain statuettes, spectacularly overcomplicated Art Nouveau vases, Rosenthal crockery, and the odd piece of Moser glass.
✉ **Maiselova 9,**

Josefov ☎ 22 31 98 16
Ⓜ Staroměstská
🕓 9am-7pm

Antique Gallery & Numismatika (5, C2)
The bare-bones name belies the wealth of collectibles inside. The Gallery does a good line in early-20th-century Russian icons, and has also stockpiled decent numbers of old coins, pocket-watches and Art Nouveau perfume bottles.
✉ **Pohořelec 9, Hradčany** ☎ **20 51 42 87** Ⓜ **Malostranská, then tram 22 or 23 to Pohořelec** 🕓 9am-6pm

Bric à Brac (7, B7)
Shop #2 of a two-shop franchise, this branch is dedicated to the Art of Deco. Old jewellery, distinctive glassware and porcelain dogs vie for the cluttered display space with old movie cameras and typewriters (some with a hungry *Naked Lunch* look about them). Shop #1 (also at Týnská 7) has less-specialised knick-knacks.
✉ **Týnská 7, Staré Město** ☎ **24 81 57 63** Ⓜ **Náměstí Republiky** 🕓 **10am-6pm**

Eduard Čapek (3, C9)
The Čapek clan have lovingly operated their bric-a-brac shop since 1911 and nothing has ever been thrown away, including the dust. Among the odds and ends are rusty typewriters, rolling pins, cracked porcelain cups and bolts that would make Frankenstein's dad weep. In the 1960s, the Czech Academy of Sciences even unearthed a valuable old engraving here of a Russian tsar.
✉ **Dlouhá 32, Josefov** Ⓜ **Náměstí Republiky** 🕓 **Mon-Fri 10am-6pm**

U Zlatého Kohouta (7, F4) A labour of love by the owner, who buys and restores antique violins, double basses and cellos to sell or just to add to his own collection. Some wonderful violins that individually date from the late 18th century up to the late 1990s hang from the rafters like polished bats, and crowd over several tables.
✉ **Michalská 3, Staré Město** ☎ **24 21 28 74** Ⓜ **Můstek** 🕓 **Mon-Fri 10am-noon & 1-6pm**

MUSIC

AghaRTA Jazz Centrum (3, K10)
Inside the esteemed AghaRTA club is a selection of the best and latest Czech and world jazz CDs for the purist to drool over. Pick up some Miles Davis and Pat Metheny and let your stereo juggle them with the latest from regular Prague performers like Jiří Stivín and Luboš Andršt.
✉ **Krakovská 5, Nové Město** ☎ **22 21 12 75** Ⓜ **Muzeum** 🕓 **7pm-midnight**

Bazar (3, K10)
Tellingly, the display of secondhand CDs here begins with Abba and ends with ZZ Top; it's also got Deep Purple's entire back-catalogue. But Gorillaz and Weezer are in there too, as are Czech artists, jazz and country noises, and soundtracks. Average CD price is about 360Kč.
✉ **Krakovská 4, Nové Město** ☎ **0602 313 730** Ⓜ **Muzeum** 🕓 **Mon-Fri 10am-6pm**

Bontonland (3, G8)
This music 'megastore' downstairs in Koruna Palace, services all your Top 10 needs and simultaneously covers jazz, classical, dance and heavy metal. It has a large Playstation

Velvet Underground Revolution

What do a Czech political campaign and the noises emitted by Reed, Cale and Co have in common? Well, Velvet Underground's music reportedly made inspirational listening for Václav Havel and fellow dissidents during communist rule. Havel finally met his idol when he interviewed Reed for *Rolling Stone* in 1990 and a bond was established between the one-time anti-establishment figures, leading to subsequent get-togethers. Havel was given a special performance by Reed at a 1998 White House function, and the pair (aided by Madeleine Albright) allegedly interrupted a 1997 gig at New York's famed Knitting Factory by talking too loudly.

arena and Internet access.
✉ **Václavské náměstí 1, Nové Město** ☎ 24 47 30 80 Ⓜ **Můstek** ◷ Mon-Sat 9am-8pm, Sun 10am-7pm

Diskoduck (7, E2)
Play 'spot the Czech DJ' at this 12" dance vinyl specialist tucked away in a courtyard off Karlova. You'll find plenty of your favourite techno, trance and house singles and remixes here. Diskoduck also sells turntables, portable mixers and other DJ-ing gear.
✉ **Karlova 12, Staré Město** ☎ 22 22 16 96 Ⓜ **Staroměstská** ◷ noon-7pm

Maximum Underground (7, E4)
In an arcade off Jilská, this retail catalogue of up-to-the-minute music styles has indie, punk, drum'n'bass, trance, trip hop, acid jazz, ska and Afro-beats, to mention a few stylised genres. Body piercing and tattoos are available next door.
✉ **L1, Jilská 22, Staré Město** ☎ 628 40 09 Ⓜ **Můstek; Staroměstská** ◷ Mon-Sat 11am-7pm, Sun 1-7pm

Music Lines (3, E1)
Air guitarists can stock up on Joe Satriani and Led Zeppelin notations for the day they finally learn how to play guitar; others can browse piano and drums sheet music. Styles include classical, pop and metal.
✉ **Saská 3, Malá Strana** ☎ 57 53 45 29 Ⓜ **Malostranská** ◷ Mon-Fri 10am-6pm, Sat 10am-4pm

Philharmonia (7, A4)
Sample the classics at this superbly stocked store, where you'll find the work of top Czech composers Dvořák, Janáček and Haas. You'll also find Czech jazz and folk music, crooners and marching bands. Eclectic inclusions pop up when least expected, like Kool & The Gang marooned among the world music.
✉ **Pařížská 13, Josefov** ☎ 232 40 60 Ⓜ **Staroměstská** ◷ 10am-6pm

Široký Dvůr (5, C3)
Let the knowledgeable Pavel recommend some contemporary Czech pop, classical or jazz strains, or perhaps some of the newly interpreted folk music

that's catching the ears of younger audiences.
✉ **Loretánské náměstí 4, Hradčany** ☎ 20 51 54 03 e www.cdmusic .cz Ⓜ **Malostranská**, then tram 22 or 23 to **Pohořelec** ◷ Tues-Sun 10am-1pm & 2-6pm

Supraphon (3, H8)
What at first appears to be just a small CD counter turns out to be a small CD counter with a huge selection of classical music, all of it catalogued in the heavy folders lined up on the countertop.
✉ **Palackého 1, Nové Město** ☎ 24 94 87 25 Ⓜ **Národní třída** ◷ Mon-Fri 9am-7pm, Sat 9am-1pm

Trio Music Shop
(7, B4) Trio is devoted to classical, Czech jazz and regional folk recordings. Pick up your favourite Mozart or Dvořák CD, or get folky and delve into Moravian outlaw songs or Wallachian drinking tunes.
✉ **U Radnice 5, Josefov** ☎ 232 25 83 Ⓜ **Staroměstská** ◷ Mon-Fri 10am-7pm, Sat-Sun 10am-6pm

All tastes are catered for, from pop, punk and drum'n'bass to classical violin.

BOOKS

Academia Bookshop (3, H9) Mislaid your copy of *Handbook of Vegetable Pests*? Someone made off with *Phytocartographical Synthesis of the Czech Republic*? Get replacements at Academia, which has a massive range of science titles upstairs – the bulk are in Czech but English-language books are scattered throughout. Downstairs are kid's books, classics and cultural guides.
⊠ **Václavské náměstí 34, Nové Město** ☎ **24 22 35 11** Ⓜ **Můstek** ⊘ **Mon-Fri 9am-8pm, Sat-Sun 10am-7pm**

Anagram (7, B7) Excellent English-language bookshop, with horizontal stacks of translated Czech works, new fiction, European history, philosophy/religion, architecture/art, kiddies' books, travel and more. Seek out the remainders section for some cheaper-than-usual buys on a range of topics.
⊠ **Týn Court 4, Staré Město** ☎ **24 89 57 37** Ⓜ **Náměstí Republiky** ⊘ **Mon-Sat 10am-8pm, Sun 10am-6pm**

Big Ben (7, B8) Well-stocked and very helpful English-language bookshop, with shelves devoted to Prague reference books (history, architecture, guides), travel, children's literature, science fiction, poetry and new-release nonfiction/fiction. Various magazines and newspapers are also at hand, as are pulp fiction paperbacks for those who prefer Koontz to Kundera.
⊠ **Malá Štupartská 5,**

A Multi-Story City

Prague has inspired the imagination of many Czech authors and bookish visitors. The ghost of Franz Kafka undoubtedly haunts the most claustrophobic of city laneways, in keeping with the smothering, obstacle-laden spirit of *The Castle* and *The Trial*. Another Czech who prefers the less-lit path is Milan Kundera, who set *The Unbearable Lightness of Being* here.

Inveterate moocher Bruce Chatwin made Josefov the landscape of his novella about a porcelain collector, *Utz*. And current Czech President Václav Havel began his writing career as resident playwright of the Theatre on the Balustrade – check out his inspirational collection of early 1990s speeches and writings, *The Art of the Impossible*.

Staré Město ☎ **24 82 65 65** Ⓜ **Náměstí Republiky** ⊘ **Mon-Fri 9am-6.30pm, Sat-Sun 10am-5pm**

Globe (3, K5) Popular haunt of the backpacking literati, with the inviting cafe out back a good place to peruse your purchases, or just sip coffee and furrow your forehead in that distinctly highbrow way. On offer here is lots of new fiction and nonfiction, translations of Czech scribblers, and English magazines. Big selection of trashy secondhand novels.
⊠ **Pštrossova 6, Nové Město** ☎ **24 91 62 64** Ⓜ **Karlovo Náměstí** ⊘ **10am-midnight**

Kanzelsberger (3, H9) Kanzelsberger has a good selection of translations of Czech authors, including Václav Havel's plays and prose, and sundry English-language novels and travel guides to leaf through.
⊠ **Václavské náměstí 42, Nové Město** ☎ **24 21 73 35** Ⓜ **Muzeum**

⊘ **Mon-Sat 8am-7pm, Sun 9am-7pm**

Prospero (7, C8) Loitering in a passageway backstage of Celetná ulice is this theatre literature specialist, where knowledgeable staff will guide you to new and secondhand tomes on dramatic happenings in the Czech Republic, plus thespian tapes, videos and CDs. The assortment of magazines includes the Theatre Institute's detailed and informative monthly, *Czech Theatre*.
⊠ **Celetná 17, Staré Město** ☎ **24 80 91 56** Ⓜ **Náměstí Republiky** ⊘ **Mon-Fri 10am-7pm**

U knihomola (4, F9) Sizeable bookshop catering to the pursuit of education via language books and tapes, dictionaries, tomes on the arts, and teacher's resources. A good range of classic literature, children's books and guidebooks.
⊠ **Mánesova 79, Vinohrady** ☎ **627 77 67** Ⓜ **Jiřího Z Poděbrad** ⊘ **Mon-Fri 11am-7pm**

FOOD & DRINK

Cellarius (3, J9)
On sale are over 1500 fine wines, courtesy of grape-stained feet as close as France, Italy and Spain, and as far afield as California and South Africa. There's another branch at Budečská 29, Vinohrady.
✉ **Lucerna Passage, Štěpánská 61, Nové Město** ☎ **24 21 09 79**
e **www.cellarius.cz**
Ⓜ **Muzeum** ◷ Mon-Sat 9.30am-9pm, Sun 3-8pm

Country Life (7, E5)
This bulk health-food off-shoot of the popular vegie restaurant experiences lots of through-traffic due to its deliciously healthy organic juices, grains and other produce. Could easily claim Prague's biggest range of soy salamis.
✉ **Melantrichova 15, Staré Město** ☎ **24 21 33 66** Ⓜ **Můstek**
◷ Mon-Thurs 8.30am-7pm, Fri 8.30am-4pm, Sun 11am-6pm

Fruits de France
(3, G10) Francophiles will break out the Pierrot costumes after visiting this consumables shop and its stash of Crème de Pêches liqueur and *moutarde* Dijon. There's also a *fromage* and *pain* section, lots of *vin*, and fresh fruit and vegies.
✉ **Jindřišská 9, Nové Město** ☎ **24 22 03 04** Ⓜ **Můstek** ◷ Mon-Wed & Fri 9.30am-6.30pm, Thurs 11.30am-6.30pm, Sat 9.30am-1pm

Havelská Market
(7, F5) To the untrained eye, long-established Havelská Market can look like a tourist-trampled bazaar where shoppers snap up Pinocchio marionettes and enough over-priced trinkets to embarrass all their friends. But the self-sufficient should check out the fresh fruit and vegies, and snacks like yoghurt-coated walnuts.
✉ **Havelská, Staré Město** Ⓜ **Můstek**
◷ 8am-6pm

J+J Mašek & Zemanová (2, E5)
Peddlers of fine foods to fine foodies with empty cupboards and rumbling tummies. Salamis dangle temptingly in the front window, and there are fresh dips, cheeses, fish and ham.
✉ **Karmelitská 30, Malá Strana** Ⓜ **Malostranská** ◷ Mon-Fri 8am-6pm, Sat 8am-noon

Memories of Africa
(7, B9) For the heavy-lidded with caffeine on the brain. Teleports beans in from Ethiopia, Burundi, Kenya, Guatemala, Costa Rica, India and Indonesia, collectively producing a heady smell sensation. Also trades in a range of teas.
✉ **Rybná, cnr of**

Jakubská, Staré Město
☎ **0603 441 434**
Ⓜ **Náměstí Republiky**
◷ 10am-7pm

Monarch (3, G6)
This vino emporium has an excellent range of Czech wines, plus international vintages from South Africa, California and Austria. Hard-to-get Australian wines are also available.
✉ **Na Perštýně 15, Staré Město** ☎ **24 23 96 03** Ⓜ **Národní třída**
◷ 10am-7pm

Pivní Galerie (4, C9)
Some think Czech beer begins and ends with Pilsener Urquell, but a visit to the tasting room at Pivní Galerie should set them right. Here you can sample and buy the liquid output of all the Czech Republic's 30-plus microbreweries. Bring an extra bladder.
✉ **U Průhonu 9, Holešovice** ☎ **20 87 06 13** Ⓜ **Nádraží Holešovice**
◷ Mon-Fri 10am-8pm, Sat 10am-3pm

Roman Kindl (3, K8)
Small but hearty selection of biodynamic foods to keep your yin from throwing a hissy-fit every time

If your liver needs a breather, head to Country Life...

Markets in the Air

Prague has a few open-air markets to scatter money in, most of them open daily (some closed Sunday) from early morning to dusk. The most prominent (and priciest) is the food and trinket emporium on **Havelská** (7, F5; see pic left), which started life as a collective of specialist markets for German merchants around 1230.

Less-distinguished but less-expensive markets, where cheap clothes elbow mounds of perfume, alcohol and toys, include the stalls at **Florenc** (3, C14), the vendors near Hradčanská metro (4, D6) at **Dejvice**, and the commercial sprawl at **Bubenské nábřeží** (4, C9).

your yang has a burger with the lot. Vegetarians will find decent takeaway snacks, and there's also the associated herbal medicines and cosmetics place next door.
⊠ **Řeznická 21, Nové Město** ☎ **0603 504 240** Ⓜ **Muzeum**
◷ Mon-Fri 9am-6pm

Tesco (3, H6)
A descent into Tesco's basement supermarket is as much an audition for *Survivor* as a shopping trip, with points awarded for evading elderly folk wiggling their carts around, and aggressively self-possessed couples oblivious to everything except the next item on their list. That said, it has most edibles inexpensively covered.
⊠ **Národní 26, Nové Město** ☎ **22 00 31 11** Ⓜ **Národní třída**
◷ Mon-Fri 7am-9pm, Sat 8am-8pm, Sun 9am-7pm

FOR CHILDREN

Dětský Dům (7, E8)
A mall for mites, often filled with the comforting sounds of new toys being bashed to smithereens. Dispenses stuff like carnival masks and video games, as well as kids' 'fashion' and maternity wear for the expectant.
⊠ **Na příkopě 15, Nové Město** ☎ **72 14 24 01** Ⓜ **Můstek**
◷ Mon-Sat 9.30am-8pm, Sun 10am-6pm

HRAS (3, H9)
Got a child who's driving you crazy? Buy them an intricate Czech wooden or wire puzzle and sit back to watch the frustration build. There are also plenty of board games, cards and assorted fun to scoop up.
⊠ **Rokoko Passage,**

Václavské náměstí 38, Nové Město ☎ **24 22 84 53** Ⓜ **Muzeum**
◷ Mon-Fri 9am-8pm, Sat 10am-3pm

Miletos Toys (3, G6)
Friendly place covering pretty much all young'un requirements. Popular items include finger puppets, marionettes and the Czech icon, 'Mole'. The store has no signage, but you'll find it next to Restaurant Svět.
⊠ **Husova 1, Staré Město** ☎ **22 22 01 921** Ⓜ **Národní třída**
◷ Mon-Thurs 10am-7pm, Fri-Sat 10.30am-7pm, Sun 11am-7pm

Obchod U Sv Jiljí (7, E4) You'll find handmade marionettes in all

manner of dress and expression sitting patiently around this shop, waiting to be adopted by young parents. Some of the models look disturbingly like Inspector Clousseau.
⊠ **Jilská 7, Staré Město** ☎ **24 23 26 95** Ⓜ **Můstek** ◷ 10am-7pm

Sparkys (7, E7)
Huge toy store, with stuffed animals from small to extra-huge, Czech toys like wooden puzzles and marionettes, model cars, computer games, sports paraphernalia, and the mandatory doll-with-an-infuriating-giggle.
⊠ **Havířská 2, Staré Město** ☎ **24 23 93 09** Ⓜ **Můstek** ◷ Mon-Sat 10am-7pm, Sun 10am-6pm

SPECIALIST STORES

Blue Green Golf Shop (6, B1)
The term 'golf fashion' is arguably an oxymoron, but beyond argument is the fact that you'll get plenty of it in this shop, plus clubs from Cobra, Pro Kennex and Wilson, and all the accessories golfers require.
⊠ Balbínova 8, Vinohrady ☎ 22 82 62 53 Ⓜ Náměstí Míru ☺ Mon-Fri 9am-6pm

Botanicus (7, B7)
Products made from natural ingredients roam free-range in this great aroma-infused shop, the place to go when you run out of green tea, bath oils, wild thyme syrup, handmade paper, or pumice on a string – they've also anticipated an upcoming trend in wire-and-walnut necklaces.
⊠ Týn Court 3, Staré Město ☎ 24 89 54 46 Ⓜ Náměstí Republiky ☺ 10am-7pm

Electrocity (3, J10)
Useful if you need some mobile phone or CD player accessories, or if you suddenly decide you're in the market for a video or digital camera, a personal organiser, a new razor, or a 70cm Grundig to replace the flatscreen you forgot to fold into your suitcase.
⊠ Vaclavské náměstí 58, Nové Město ☎ 96 15 81 34 Ⓜ Muzeum ☺ 9am-9pm

Hubbub & Sons
(7, B9) This booth/shop is a big importer of pipes, mainly from India, though a few Czech ceramic pipes are also at hand. Flung aesthetically around the place are groovy original tie-dyes, hats, bangles, bracelets, bells and bongos. You may have heard you can score dope here – you can't, so leave the staff in peace.
⊠ Jakubská 8, Staré Město ☎ 24 81 34 41 Ⓜ Náměstí Republiky ☺ Apr-Oct 10am-10pm, Nov-Mar 10am-8pm

Hudy Sport (3, G6)
One of the half-dozen Hudy Sport shops around Prague providing advice and reasonably priced outdoor equipment to those who prefer nature to a nature strip. Good array of quality hiking boots, backpacks, camping gear, skis, even the odd kayak or two.
⊠ Na Perštýně 14, Staré Město ☎ 24 21 86 00 Ⓜ Národní třída ☺ Mon-Fri 9am-7.30pm, Sat 9am-1pm

Městské Mapkupectví (7, C3)
Map shop run by Prague municipality, with an extensive range of local and international touring maps and atlases, plus regional hiking maps. For an unusual but clear perspective on the city, pick up a copy of *Praha ortofotomapa*, which maps Prague through aerial photography.
⊠ Žatecká 2, Staré Město ☎ 24 48 24 80 Ⓜ Staroměstská ☺ Mon-Fri 8am-6pm

Nomad (3, J9)
At first peek Nomad appears dedicated to striking handmade Oriental rugs. But a wander through the gallery reveals other authentic items such as Tibetan antiques, Burmese statuettes, and turquoise and lapis lazuli jewellery from Nepal and Afghanistan.
⊠ Lucerna Passage, Štěpánská 61, Nové Město ☎ 96 23 63 43 Ⓜ Muzeum ☺ Mon-Fri 10am-7pm, Sat 10am-6pm

U Tří Stupňů (3, G6)
Small local perfumery, where you can get a spray from Brut, smell Calvin for Eternity, grapple with Estee's Intuition, sniff out Hugo Boss, get a dose of Christian's Poison, or let out a Joop!.
⊠ Uhelný trh 3, Staré Město ☎ 24 23 43 42 Ⓜ Můstek ☺ Mon-Fri 7am-7.30pm, Sat-Sun 8am-6pm

In the Hubbub, put that in your pipe and smoke it...

places to eat

Lately there's been an explosion (a very nicely flavoured one) of ethnic restaurants in Prague, meaning your diet can stretch beyond standard Czech fare whenever you'd like it to. Don't take typical Czech cuisine for granted, though, as there are plenty of restaurants and pubs serving top-quality, often cheap local food, or creatively adapting it with a fresh international approach in mind.

Meal Costs

The prices in this chapter indicate the cost of a two-course meal with one drink for one person.

$	up to 260Kč
$$	260-479Kč
$$$	480-740Kč
$$$$	over 740Kč

Richard Nebesky

The average Czech day includes breakfast *(snídaně)* with bread *(chléb)*, cheese, ham, eggs and coffee, eaten at home or at one of the many, simple *bufety* (self-service places). Lunch (the main meal of the day) or dinner *(oběd)* consists of soup *(polévka)* and often the ubiquitous dumplings *(knedlo)*, sauerkraut *(zelo)* and roast pork *(vepřo)*. Other favoured items, particularly in pubs, include pork sausages *(buřt)*, goulash *(guláš)* and the delicious *svíčková na smetaně* (roast beef and bread dumplings in sour-cream sauce with cranberries).

Less pleasurable is an extra-large serving of waiter indifference, regarded as a professional qualification in some places. But this isn't always the natural state of affairs and you have the option of either trying to break through the facade with some Czech words or good humour, or (as most do) just ignoring it. It'll be harder to ignore the cigarette smoke that clouds most establishments, except in many eateries at lunchtime when the custom is to refrain from puffing until lunch is finished.

A place calling itself a *restaurace* should be a cheaper restaurant, but often isn't. A *vinárna* is a wine bar that will mainly serve bite-sized items but can have a full menu. A *kavárna* is a cafe, which in Prague usually means alcohol prevails as much as coffee and food is restricted to snacks and sweets. Restaurant hours vary markedly, as do kavárna times, with many staying open late most nights; pubs are usually open from 11am to 11pm.

Chris Mellor

Cramming in for an al fresco meal

HRADČANY

Cafe Himalaya
(2, J2) $
Vegetarian
You don't come here for the view – windswept asphalt surrounded by concrete-block dorms. Rather, you stumble across it after attending a club or losing your way from Petřín Hill. This tiny place serves vegie curries, pasta and pizza.
✉ **Chaloupeckého, Strahov** ☎ **33 35 35 94** Ⓜ **Dejvická, then bus 143, 149 or 217 to Chaloupeckého** ☺ **Mon-Thurs 3pm-5am, Fri-Sun 3pm-3am** Ⓥ

Café Poet (2, C2) $$
Cafe
Tourist cafe with an outdoor area set in a courtyard of the castle. Pricey, but a little less so than similar eateries. Re-energise yourself with sausages, pasta or salads. Plenty of sundaes to keep the kids occupied.
✉ **Na Baště** ☎ **24 37 35 99** Ⓜ **Malostranská** ☺ **10am-6pm**

Lví Dvůr
(2, A2) $$-$$$
Traditional & Modern Czech
This prime-time tourist and corporate personality hangout is at the western end of Royal Garden. It's full of perfected traditional ambience, and it has a thing for piglet meat – a 4-5kg squealer costs 4500Kč.
✉ **U Prašného mostu 6** ☎ **24 37 23 61** Ⓜ **Malostranská, then tram 22, 23 to Pražský hrad** ☺ **10am-2am** ♿

Malý Buddha (5, C3) $
Vegetarian, Asian
Tea-and-vegetables temple transplanted from the Orient complete with a Buddhist shrine, and mobbed nightly by devotees. Has 'healing wines' and teas to accompany the plant chow. Also serves crab, shark and crocodile. Credit cards unpalatable.
✉ **Úvoz 46** ☎ **20 51 38 94** Ⓜ **Malostranská, then tram 22 or 23 to Pohořelec** ☺ **Tues-Sun 1-10.30pm** ♿ Ⓥ

Oživlé Dřevo
(5, D3) $$$
Modern Czech
Wine and dine someone special or just an enigmatic passing stranger in this upmarket, cushion-filled hall at the base of Strahov Monastery. Try the marinated beef or Malosol caviar. Handsome youngsters go for the windblown look on the terrace.
✉ **Strahovské nádvoří 1** ☎ **20 51 72 74** Ⓜ **Malostranská, then tram 22 or 23 to Pohořelec** ☺ **10.30am-11pm**

Sate (5, C2) $
Indonesian
Budget fare in pseudo-authentic Indonesian surroundings, with a basic menu that appears to have changed little over many a digestive aeon. Offers good standards like *mie & nasi goreng, ayam blado* (chicken with paprika sauce and egg) and its vegetarian sibling *telur blado*.
✉ **Pohořelec 3** ☎ **20 51 45 52** Ⓜ **Malostranská, then tram 22 or 23 to Pohořelec** ☺ **11am-10pm** ♿ Ⓥ

U císařů (5, B4) $$
Traditional Czech
Regularly invaded by massive tour groups who come to eat under the emperor portraits. You can get some quality game here – for a bit of everything get the 'Emperor skewer', which has a number of animals impaled on it.
✉ **Loretánská 5** ☎ **20 51 84 84** Ⓜ **Malostranská** ☺ **11am-midnight** ♿

U zlaté hrušky
(5, A4) $$$-$$$$
Traditional Czech
Low-ceilinged, wood-panelled affair serving outstanding traditional fare from its huge menu, like snail slices in red oil and baked duck legs. Some meals, like lobster tails or marinated rabbit, need to be ordered in advance.
✉ **Nový Svět 3** ☎ **20 51 53 56** Ⓜ **Malostranská, then tram 22 or 23 to Pohořelec** ☺ **11.30am-3pm & 6pm-midnight**

The view from Oživlé Dřevo will blow you away.

JOSEFOV

Barock (3, C6) $$-$$$
Breakfast & Brunch
Breezy place on fashion-swept Pařížská, with side-walk space and a stylish interior dotted with arty photos and people in black. Offers a decent range of cocktails and cig-arillos with which to per-fect your measured pose, and a menu filled with eggs, salads, baguettes and pastries.
✉ **Pařížská 24** ☎ **232 92 21** Ⓜ **Staroměstská** ◷ 8.30am-1am; break-fast served Mon-Fri 8.30am-11.30am, Sat-Sun 10am-4pm

Chez Marcel (3, C8) $$
French & Breakfast
Spacious, mustard-walled place with a cruisy tiled-cafe feel, friendly service and lots of ashtrays to fill. There's a long salad list and a melt-in-your-mouth ratatouille, but the huge omelettes win the food fight: try wrapping your mouth around *vejce se šunkou a sýrem* (eggs with ham and cheese).
✉ **Haštalská 12** ☎ **22 31 56 76** Ⓜ **Náměstí Republiky** ◷ 8am-late ♿ Ⓥ

Franz Kafka Café (3, D6) $
Cafe
Slurp *káva* surrounded by brooding shots of Prague in the wood-panelled front room, or flee into a dark rear alcove to ponder life's trials over a *pivo* and some quark. Also serves juices and teas, plus small tasters like goulash for 95Kč and ice cream from 50Kč.
✉ **Široká 12** Ⓜ **Staro-městská** ◷ 10am-10pm

Jeruzalem (3, C5) $$-$$$
Kosher
Light and bright kosher restaurant with beach-house pastels looking for a sea breeze. Munch break-fasts (180-250Kč), vegie specials, and treats like salt pancakes and ice cream.
✉ **Břehová 5** ☎ **24 81 20 01** Ⓜ **Staroměstská** ◷ 8am-11pm ♿ Ⓥ

Jewel of India (3, C6) $$-$$$
Indian
Serves up fantastic North Indian cuisine in formal but unoppressive surroundings. Lots of curry and vegetarian specialities expertly dished out – the *tandoori murgh* is outstanding, and the *dhal* has quite a zing to it.
✉ **Pařížská 20** ☎ **24 81 10 10** Ⓜ **Staro-městská** ◷ 11.30am-3pm & 5.30-11pm ♿ Ⓥ

Orange Moon (3, C8) $$
South-East Asian
Newish sub-ground haven for Thai, Burmese and Indian cuisines. The menu goes for safe but tasty options like stir fries, noo-dles, *biryani* and curries (just-right portions), and gives you an accurate chilli index to select your own level of spice comfort.
✉ **Rámová 5** ☎ **232 51 19** Ⓜ **Náměstí Republiky** ◷ 11.30am-11.30pm Ⓥ

Pravda (3, C6) $$$-$$$$
Modern Czech
For something special, choose a formal white cloth-covered table, enjoy the menu's top choice (pan-fried sea bass), then apply the motto of the bar: 'Walk in, dance out'.
✉ **Pařížská 17** ☎ **232 62 03** Ⓜ **Staroměstská** ◷ noon-1am

Švejk (7, A4) $$
Beer Hall
Not the most authentic pub-restaurant you'll find, rather one that has a bit of a self-conscious air about it. But you can get some de-cent Czech staples here, like roast lamb in sherry sauce.
✉ **Široká 20** ☎ **24 81 39 64** Ⓜ **Staroměstská** ◷ 11am-11pm

Dealing With 'Bill'
'Bill' can be a fractious fellow in Prague restaurants. Often he ends up costing you more than you expect, and often you don't understand what he's trying to tell you. Here are some hints on coping with him.

Double-check your bill carefully as there are a few people working in Prague's eateries who either failed mathematics in school or got top marks in the 'over-charging' business elective. Stuff you'd take for grant-ed back home often comes at a price in Prague – wave away items you didn't order or don't want. Finally, be aware that many places have a cover charge, and that tips can be included in your final amount.

MALÁ STRANA

Bohemia Bagel
(2, H5) $
Cafe
Two-branch Internet cafe that has decided it's on a good thing with the holy rolls, fine for a quick stomach fix. You can get sandwich bagels (if you're feeling oxymoronic), bagel 'melts', or bagels with specialty cream cheeses. It also offers a passable vegetarian chilli.
✉ **Újezd 16** ☎ **57 31 06 94** Ⓜ **Národní třída, then tram 22, 23 or 57 to Újezd** ◷ **Mon-Fri 7am-midnight, Sat-Sun 8am-midnight**

Caffè-Ristorante
Italia (2, D3) $$
Italian
Offers hearty Italian in generic surroundings, perhaps a tad too hearty to immediately tackle the nearby climb to the castle. And don't expect accordion music – you're more likely to hear home-boy rap when the waiters get restless.
✉ **Nerudova 17**
☎ **57 53 28 18**
Ⓜ **Malostranská**
◷ **9am-11pm**

Gitanes (2, E4) $$-$$$
Mediterranean
Gitanes looks as if the contents of an entire Mediterranean village have been swept up by a tornado and deposited at random inside its walls. It's impossible not to feel cheery here, with the bright colours, good selection of seafood and pasta, and wine from Croatia and Bosnia-Hercegovina.
✉ **Tržiště 7** ☎ **57 53 01 63** Ⓜ **Malostranská** ◷ **11am-11pm**

Hostinec U kocoura
(2, D4) $
Beer Hall
One of Malá Strana's more subdued beer halls where Czech groups predominate in a low-key way, making for a relaxing, commotion-free beer after all that hurly-burly sightseeing. Serves all the traditional staples.
✉ **Nerudova 2**
☎ **57 53 01 07**
Ⓜ **Malostranská**
◷ **11am-11.30pm**

Izinkan (2, D2) $$
Japanese
Izinkan has tried hard to

create an upstairs oasis with pebble-strewn steps, thatchwork, traditional rock garden and terrific food. At dinnertime you can get seven courses from 560Kč, and there's a Japanese-style buffet Saturday from 11am-3pm.
✉ **Nerudova 36**
☎ **57 53 30 82**
Ⓜ **Malostranská**
◷ **noon-10pm** Ⓥ

Kampa Park
(3, E2) $$$$
Modern Czech, Seafood
Exclusive restaurant/bar complex claiming the northern end of Kampa, giving its clientele magical views of the river, particularly at night. Serves top-class international food and wine to famous types who then get listed on the back of a brochure, obviously to create some much-needed I've-eaten-there-too rivalry in the celebrity world. For a good table, book at least three-four days ahead.
✉ **Na Kampě 8b**
☎ **57 53 26 85**
Ⓜ **Malostranská**
◷ **11.30am-late** Ⓥ

Pálffy Palác
(3, C1) $$$-$$$$
French
The decor is substantial and luxurious but the menu is small and choosy, so you can't make too many faux pas if trying to impress someone in this favourite haunt of embassy diplomats and parliamentarians. The Francophile-slanted food is along the lines of ostrich with walnut sauce.
✉ **Valdštejnská 14**
☎ **57 53 05 22**
Ⓜ **Malostranská**
◷ **10am-midnight**

Waiter, There's a View in My Soup
At **Restaurant Zlatá Praha** (náměstí Curieových 43/5; 3, B6; $$$-$$$$; ☎ 24 88 99 14), you can gaze upon the spires of Prague from the 9th-floor of the Hotel Inter-Continental. For park-views, try tucking into stuffed salmon at **Restaurant Nebozízek** (Petřínské sady 411; 2, H2; $$; ☎ 57 31 53 29).

Hanavský pavilón (Letenské sady 173; 3, A4; $$$; ☎ 33 32 36 41) is a neo-baroque 1891 pavilion with good seafood and views. **U Zlaté studně** (U Zlaté Studně 4; 2, C5; $$$; ☎ 57 53 33 22), in the hotel of the same name, has a fantastic vista. Highest of them all is the **Tower Restaurant** (Mahlerovy sady 1; 4, E9; $$; ☎ 67 00 57 78) in Žižkov's TV Tower.

Cafe Culture to a Tea...

Since the mid-1990s, a number of smokeless, tranquil tearooms *(čajovny)* have won popularity in Prague. **Dobrá čajovna** (Boršov 2; 3, G4; $) has an entrancing Arabic feel and dozens of Oriental blends.

Turecká čajovna a dobroty (Úvoz 1; 2, D2; $; ☎ 71 73 48 90; see pic left) has Turkish rugs and mock pillars. **Čajovna pod stromem čajovým** (Mánesova 55; 6, B5; $; ☎ 22 25 10 45) has a shisha and lots of teas.

U zeleného čaje (Nerudova 19; 2, D3; $; ☎ 57 53 00 27) is a good pit-stop for a refreshing brew. **Modrá čajovna** (Jánský vršek 8; 2, E2; $; ☎ 0602 176 355) is in a peaceful Malá Strana side-street courtyard, while **Růžová čajovna** (Růžová 8; 3, G11; $; ☎ 22 24 58 94) has a more modern whitewashed interior, plus live music, and lots of tea and tea-ware on sale upstairs.

Pasha (3, C2) $$$
Middle Eastern, Mediterranean
Exotic blazing-red interior sees lots of expats looking for a good-food night out. They shouldn't be disappointed either, as there are many excellent Turkish- and Lebanese-influenced meals to choose from, with a fair division between vegetarian and carnivorous dishes.
✉ **U lužického semináře 23** ☎ 57 53 24 34 Ⓜ **Malostranská**
🕐 **Tues-Sun 11.30am-11pm** **V**

Rybářský klub (3, G2) $$
Seafood
Rybářský's modest premises, with plain wooden benches, are actually a down-to-earth front for some classy cooking of fish, particularly the freshwater variety. Trout and carp are quickly and deliciously prepared; one of the best dishes is pike perch in basil. Don't forget to order a glass of Czech or Moravian wine too.
✉ **U Sovových mlýnů 1** ☎ 57 53 42 00

Ⓜ **Národní třída, then tram 22, 23 or 57 to Hellichova**
🕐 **noon-11pm**

St Nicholas Café (2, E4) $
Cafe
Compact lower-level cafe with the soot-stained look of a chimney in parts. Popular with a chatty young Czech/foreigner crowd who bulk up on 'Woodchopper's steak' and later in the afternoon turn their attention to whisky rather than coffee.
✉ **Tržiště 10** ☎ 57 53 02 04 Ⓜ **Malostranská**
🕐 **2pm-late**

Sushi Bar (3, J1) $-$$
Japanese
The Sushi Bar is a small, bright place with the interior colour of a hollowed-out lime, serving fantastic sushi to nibble inside or run away with. This neighbourhood institution also has good soups from 40Kč, and stocks of sake for the thirsty.
✉ **Zborovská 49** ☎ 0603 244 882

Ⓜ **Národní třída, then tram 6, 9, 22, 23, 57 or 58 to Újezd**
🕐 **11am-10pm** ⚹

U Bílé kuželky (3, E2) $-$$
Traditional Czech
This Czech restaurant spreads itself thin by trying to accommodate a cafe, restaurace and jazz & blues club, confusing tourists who stumble into it off Charles Bridge. The mainstream Czech cuisine includes good *svíčková* (creamy vegetable sauce with sliced meat and dumplings). Entry is off Dražického náměstí.
✉ **Míšeňská 12** ☎ 57 53 57 68 Ⓜ **Malostranská** 🕐 **11am-11pm**

U malířů (2, E5) $$$$
French, Seafood
Splendid, romantic Art-Nouveau setting in a mid-16th-century building, where you can indulge in some exemplary seafood – baked mussels, seadog Provencal, aubergine cake with crab stuffing – or Bohemian dishes like roast

duck or (imagine this one) boar terrine.

✉ **Maltézské náměstí 11** ☎ **57 53 00 00**
Ⓜ **Malostranská**
🕐 **11.30am–midnight**

U modré kachničky
(2, G5) **$$$**
Modern Czech
Grandly-styled eatery heavy on the old-elegance factor and sumptuous food, and claiming the obligatory list of well-nourished celebrities. This is the place for duck – try duck with Cumberland sauce – but there's plenty of other wild game like deer and pheasant.

✉ **Nebovidská 6**
☎ **57 32 03 08**
Ⓜ **Národní třída**, then tram 22, 23 or 57 to Hellichova 🕐 noon–4pm, 6.30-11.30pm

U sedmi Svabu
(2, D2) **$$**
Traditional Czech
The cardboard cut-out of a red-cheeked, decidedly legless knight out the front tells you pretty much all you need to know. There's lots of beer flowing here, plus lip-smacking traditional treats like pork lard with onions and apples.

✉ **Jánský vršek 14**
☎ **57 53 14 55**
Ⓜ **Malostranská**
🕐 **11am-11pm**

U tří zlatých hvězd
(2, E4) **$$**
Traditional Czech
Good traditional Czech restaurant with the dignified air of a chapel but somehow decidedly non-stuffy. Serves excellent Bohemian onion soup and a

rice dish that's a real mouthful ('Miss Zuzanska of Malá Strana'). The multilingual menu attracts lots of visitors; evenings are particularly busy.

✉ **Malostranské náměstí 8** ☎ **57 53 16 36** Ⓜ **Malostranská**
🕐 **11.30am-11pm**

U Zavěšeného Kafe
(2, D1) **$**
Cafe
Also known as the The Hanging Coffee (ask about it), this place has featured heavily in the city's artistic past and has many loyal and intelligence-brewing followers, as symbolised by the sculpture of a figure with a coffee cup for a head.

✉ **Úvoz 6**
Ⓜ **Malostranská**
🕐 **11am-midnight**

NOVÉ MĚSTO

Alcron **(3, J9)** **$$$$**
Seafood
Only two-dozen people can squeeze into this snazzy Art Deco chamber, with its Roaring Twenties murals, to enjoy seafood specialities, like marinated marlin and sauteed soft-shell crab. Don't forget to have a martini in the leopard-

print 'lounge' before sashaying in.
✉ **Radisson SAS Alcron Hotel, Štěpánská 40**
☎ **22 82 00 38**
Ⓜ **Muzeum** 🕐 Mon-Sat 5.30-10.30pm

Angel Café **(3, K5)** **$$**
Breakfast & Brunch
Not your regular big-style

cafe, but rather a minimalist, modern place with a laid-back neighbourhood feel and superb, freshly thrown-together cuisine. How does a marsala omelette with spiced potatoes sound? Or lingonberry polenta pancakes? Weekend brunch is 11am-3pm, but you

Indulge in the soft-shell shuffle at the Alcron.

should try the creative lunch menu too.

✉ Opatovická 3 ☎ 24 93 00 19, 0602 367 444 Ⓜ Národní třída
🕓 11am-3pm (Thurs-Sat 7-10pm) ♿

Branický sklípek (3, J8) $
Beer Hall
Also known as U Purk-mistra, this lively Czech pub brews its own beer and has only Czech-language menus, so if you want to eat here make sure you brush up on your culinary terms first. It's rumoured to have the best Czech vegie meals around.

✉ Vodičkova 26
☎ 22 23 05 07
Ⓜ Národní třída
🕓 Mon-Fri 9am-11pm, Sat-Sun 11am-11pm Ⓥ

Buffalo Bill's (3, J7) $$
Tex-Mex
Hombres and cowgirls pre-ferred in this downstairs bar/grill, where iconic posters and cut-outs from Hollywood Westerns try to outnumber the patrons. Serves all the regular Tex-Mex gourmet stuff like ribs, wings, steaks, burritos, tacos and nachos, all topped with liberal por-tions of country music.

✉ Vodičkova 9
☎ 24 94 86 24
Ⓜ Národní třída
🕓 High Noon-midnight

Café Louvre (3, H6) $$
Breakfast & Brunch, Cafe
Join young professionals and disoriented tourists in this one-time billiard par-lour (you can still play in the side-room) that's graced Národní for nearly a century, not counting a 44-year communist shutdown.

***

Corporate Cuisine
There are plenty of perfect places for deal-making, pro-crastinating, or plain entertaining. **Casablanca** (see below) is a fancy Kosher Moroccan restaurant that offers a three-course business menu (495Kč/person). **Restaurant Flambée** (7, F3; $$$$; Husova 5; ☎ 24 24 85 12) is an exclusive cellar retreat. Inside the Hotel Pařiž is **Café de Paris** (7, B10; $$; U Obecního domu 1; ☎ 22 19 51 95), a good place to casually impress a business connection. **Restaurant James Cook** (4, G8; $-$$; Oldřichova 14, Vyšehrad; ☎ 692 62 90) has cheap versions of meals like ostrich and kangaroo, and **Oživlé Dřevo** (5, D3; $$$; see p. 70) has a great ter-race and an upmarket Czech menu.

***

Starched-uniformed waiters serve a variety of desserts and set breakfasts; seedy types should have the *fla-mendr* (beer, goulash and a large espresso).

✉ Národní 22
☎ 24 93 09 49/12
Ⓜ Národní třída
🕓 Mon-Fri 8am-late, Sat-Sun 9am-late ♿ Ⓥ

Carioca (3, G8) $$
Thai, Traditional Czech
Combination salsa club, cocktail bar and restaurant with a much-praised Thai menu, now serving Czech meals as well after a change of ownership. The venue offers quite an eating experience: imagine you're Jonah and you've been swallowed by a small whale with a rococo rib-cage.

✉ Václavské náměstí 4
☎ 96 32 53 13
Ⓜ Můstek
🕓 11.30am-late Ⓥ

Casablanca (7, F8) $$$-$$$$
Middle Eastern
Kosher Moroccan restau-rant set up in opulent style at the end of a long pas-sageway leading from Na Příkopě through Savarin

Palace. The cooking is a hit with local food critics and businesspeople, the latter regular users of Casa-blanca's almost daily business menu (unavailable Saturday).

✉ Na Příkopě 10
☎ 24 21 05 19
Ⓜ Můstek
🕓 11.30am-midnight

Casa Mia (3, J8) $$$
Seafood
One part pizzeria, one part lavishly decorated restau-rant where fresh John Dory, sea bass and toad-fish is expertly cooked Mediterranean-style and prepared at your table. Staff tend to melt away, making it a good place for business lunches, particu-larly the expansive court-yard. Twilight bookings recommended.

✉ Vodičkova 17
☎ 96 23 82 04
Ⓜ Národní třída
🕓 11am-11pm

Dynamo (3, J5) $$
Modern Czech
Sleek eatery with good food and all the ultra-modern trimmings – wooden floor, lots of space between

tables, arty bimbo pictures, guacamole-smeared walls – attracting a well-dressed 30-something crowd. The menu is 'international', which means the combinations of foodstuffs are unpredictable.
- ✉ Pštrossova 29
- ☎ 24 93 20 20
- Ⓜ Národní Třída
- ⏰ 11.30am-midnight

Govinda Vegetarian Club (3, B11) $
Vegetarian
Simple, replenishing vegetarian dished up cafeteria-style by followers of the Hare Krishna to quite a mixture of people. The menu changes daily, with soups and salads only 15Kč, rice 20Kč and *subji* 25Kč. Everybody has to clear up after themselves, so the domestically pampered should start practising their dish-carrying technique.
- ✉ Soukenická 27
- ☎ 24 81 66 31
- Ⓜ Náměstí Republiky
- ⏰ Mon-Sat 11am-5.30pm ♿ Ⓥ

Handi (3, H6) $
Indian
East meets East at Handi, which shares its business with a Chinese restaurant upstairs. You'll find

reasonable Indian food on its brief menu. It's a good place to stuff your face with *pakoras* and *samosas* before whirling off down Národní – and it has take-away too.
- ✉ Národní 23
- ☎ 24 21 18 88
- Ⓜ Národní třída
- ⏰ 11am-midnight Ⓥ

Káva Káva Káva (3, G7) $
Cafe
Fine-coffee emporium in a snug corner of a courtyard off Národní. Another of Prague's really good, soothingly ordinary cafes where businesspeople, weary shoppers, tourists and residents alike go to just drink coffee and think or talk.
- ✉ Národní 37
- ☎ 24 22 88 62
- Ⓜ Můstek
- ⏰ Mon-Fri 7am-10pm, Sat-Sun 9am-10pm

Kavárna obecní dům (7, C10) $$
Cafe
Chandelier-littered cafe in the utterly Art-Nouveau Municipal House. Carnivores can choose from fish and other meat dishes such as a traditional Moravian plate (Prague ham, roasted garlic pork, sausage and pickled peppers); vegetarians will have to be

content with the view.
- ✉ náměstí Republiky 5
- ☎ 22 00 27 63
- Ⓜ Náměstí Republiky
- ⏰ 8am-11pm ♿

Kavárna Slavia (3, H4) $$
Cafe
Since an interior overhaul, this ex-intellectual Art-Deco haunt has resigned itself to serving overpriced fare to tourists; not much food for thought here nowadays. Still OK to sit in for a coffee and a view to the river, though pillars and the occasional tram tend to limit the vista.
- ✉ Národní 1
- ☎ 24 21 84 93
- Ⓜ Národní třída
- ⏰ 9am-11pm ♿

La Perle de Prague (4, F6) $$$$
Seafood, French
Atop the Dancing Building, this formal restaurant has sweeping views and some of the best marine concoctions in the city. If you've recently tired of seafood, try the cognac-flavoured duck liver terrine instead.
- ✉ 7th flr, Dancing Building, Rašinovo nábřeží 80
- ☎ 21 98 41 60
- Ⓜ Karlovo Náměstí
- ⏰ Mon 7-10.30pm, Tues-Sat noon-2pm & 7-10.30pm

Le Café Français (3, K8) $
Cafe
If you feel like a croissant and want to enjoy it while surrounded by authentic French voices, head for this simple, cheap cafe in the back of the Institut Français de Prague. Croissants are 15Kč and French tarts 35Kč.
- ✉ Štěpánská 35
- ☎ 22 23 31 01
- Ⓜ Muzeum
- ⏰ Mon-Fri 9am-7pm

At Kavárna Slavia, it's goodbye literati, hello latte-rati.

Le Patio
(3, H6)　　　**$$-$$$**
Breakfast & Brunch
Expensive cafe fronting a lifestyle store, decorated like the hideaway of an Arabian pirate with a flair for interior design and a penchant for light fittings. Society types meet here over baguettes and extended Continental breakfasts.
✉ **Národní 22** ☎ **24 91 80 72** Ⓜ Národní třída ⏲ Mon-Fri 8am-11pm, Sat-Sun 10am-11pm ♿

Mayur Indický Restaurant (3, J9)　**$$**
Indian
Mayur Indický has staff so friendly it makes you suspicious, and there are lots of reasonably-priced Mughlai specialities, including the wonderful-tasting *murgh Makhani* (braised chicken in a spice-infused cream sauce). There are several vegie curries (soya meat-flavoured) to choose from.
✉ **Štěpánská 63** ☎ **24 22 70 73** Ⓜ Muzeum ⏲ 11.30am-11.30pm ♿ **V**

Miyabi (3, K8)　　**$$**
Japanese
This is a highly relaxing combination of Japanese restaurant, cafe and tearoom, a good spot to settle in for a long, mouth-watering struggle with tempura, teppanyaki, sushi and *obentó* (Japanese in a box). For a virtual preview, check out the website.
✉ **Navrátilova 10** ☎ **96 23 31 02** Ⓔ www.miyabi.cz/_english/index.html Ⓜ Karlovo Náměstí ⏲ Mon-Fri 11am-11pm, Sat-Sun noon-11pm **V**

Novoměstský pivovar
(3, K8)　　　**$-$$**
Beer Hall
Brewery-restaurant complex less than a decade old that makes great beer (Novoměstský ležák) purely for the purpose of quenching the thirsts of patrons in its busy food areas. House specialities include creamy beef sirloin with dumplings, and roasted pork-knee.
✉ **Vodičkova 20** ☎ **22 23 24 18** Ⓜ Národní třída ⏲ Mon-Fri 10am-11.30pm, Sat 11.30am-11.30pm, Sun noon-10pm

Ostroff (3, J2)　　**$$$**
Italian, Modern Czech
Low-lit, suave restaurant on an isle in the Vltava; book a table in the long front room for views. Artfully splatter your white tablecloth with the remnants of ravioli stuffed with tuna, or mushroom souffle with black truffles. In the warmer months see the place transform into a cocktail bar.
✉ **Střelecký ostrov 336** ☎ **24 91 92 35** Ⓜ Národní třída ⏲ Mon-Sat noon-2pm & 7-11pm

Pizzeria Kmotra
(3, J5)　　　**$$**
Italian
The 'Godmother' proves it's nothing personal, just professional, by flinging food-topped dough around this boisterous tavern-like pizzeria. Kmotra is always packed with yabbering folk settling into booths for cocktails (like the optimistic 'Sex on the Beach') and perhaps a pizza with hazelnut chocolate cream.
✉ **V jirchářích 12** ☎ **24 91 58 09**

Ⓜ Národní třída ⏲ 11am-midnight **V**

Pod křídlem
(3, H5)　　　**$$-$$$**
Modern Czech
A world of Art Deco re-created in 1999 and frequented by business suits and elegant Národní bystanders. The staff efficiently serve platters of Czech steak, duck and rabbit prepared with an international twist.
✉ **Voršilská** ☎ **24 95 17 41** Ⓜ Národní třída ⏲ Mon-Fri 10am-midnight, Sat-Sun 11.30am-midnight

Red Room (3, K5)　**$$**
Breakfast & Brunch
The place to go when you want to see something that looks seedier than you do. Drenched in rouge, this is a popular cocktail bar at night and turns into a weekend recovery brunch venue, with eggs Benedict, eggs Scrambled etc; maintain the theme with a Bloody Mary.
✉ **Křemencova 17** ☎ **24 91 60 47** Ⓜ Národní třída ⏲ 11am-1am; brunch Sat-Sun 11am-5pm

Restaurace MD Rettigové (3, D10)　**$$**
Traditional Czech
Dishes out food in the name of Magdaleny Dobromily Rettigové, a Bohemian woman who penned a famous cookbook over 200 years ago. Apparently she was a dab hand at stuffed quail, but her best work was a mixture of duck, pork, smoked meat and cabbage.
✉ **Truhlářská 4** ☎ **22 31 44 83** Ⓜ Náměstí Republiky ⏲ 11am-11pm

Taj Mahal
(3, K11) $$-$$$
Indian
Hidden behind the National
Museum, this superb Indian
restaurant uses the spice
rack with subtlety. The chef
dotes on *rogan josh* and
the better-than-ectoplasmic
ghost passanda, but you
can't really go wrong with
any dish.
✉ **Škretova 10** ☎ **24
22 55 66** Ⓜ **Muzeum**
🕘 Mon-Sat 11.30am-
11.30pm, Sun 2.30-
10.30pm Ⓥ

TGI Friday's (7, D9) **$$**
Tex-Mex
In this paraphernalia-
stuffed parlour, the idea is
to get you greased up and
out the door as quickly as
possible. The staff wear
the silliest hats this side of
Beck, but the meals are
huge and there are sepa-
rate smoking and non-
smoking areas.
✉ **Na příkopě 27**
☎ **22 18 43 01**
Ⓜ **Náměstí Republiky**
🕘 11am-midnight
♿ Ⓥ

U Fleků (3, K5)   **$$**
Beer Hall
The 'oldest family brewery'
in Prague certainly milks
the concept, with a seating
capacity of 1200 and an
on-site museum. At least
you'll never be lonely here
while you're eating your
roast goose with potato
and bacon dumplings, such
is the never-ending crowd
– first in, best fed.
✉ **Křemencova 11**
☎ **24 91 51 18**
Ⓜ **Národní třída**
🕘 10am-11pm ♿

STARÉ MĚSTO

Bellevue (3, G4) **$$$$**
French
Formally attired Bellevue
comes with exceptional
river views and plenty of
upmarket attitude. Specialities include veal tenderloin.
Sunday is jazz brunch time,
when 795Kč will give you a
buffet and all the cham-
pagne you can guzzle; book
ahead to avoid sobriety.
✉ **Smetanovo nábřeží
18** ☎ **22 22 14 38**
Ⓜ **Národní třída**
🕘 Mon-Sat noon-3pm
& 5.30-11pm, Sun
11am-3.30pm & 7-11pm

cafe ~ cafe (3, G7) **$**
Cafe
Unimaginatively named

but classy space with a big
mirror for preening and big
windows for people-
watching. Serves good coffee, sundaes and sweets,
and lots of booze to a professionally relaxed crowd.
✉ **Rytířská 10**
☎ **24 21 05 97**
Ⓜ **Můstek** 🕘 Mon-Fri
10am-midnight, Sat-
Sun 11am-midnight

Cafe Indigo
(7, C1)   **$-$$**
Breakfast & Brunch
The food can be ordinary
at times, but it's worth
eating here just to sit
among the confused mix-
ture of trendy photos,
phallic wall-hangings,

Grab a muffin muffin at cafe ~ cafe.

Richard Nebeský

cast-iron idols and spacey
electronic music that must
be that new 'robot
cabaret'. The official brunch
menu applies on the week-
end only (11am-4pm).
✉ **Platnéřská 11**
☎ **26 20 22 47**
Ⓜ **Staroměstská**
🕘 Mon-Fri 11am-mid-
night, Sat-Sun 11am-
late ♿

Clementinum
(7, C1)   **$$**
Modern Czech
Tasty mix of Czech and
international cuisine, with
dishes like turkey fricassee,
potato gnocchi and roast
duck with Carlsbad dump-
lings sharing the menu. Has
a modern, elegant interior
with subdued colours and
unobtrusive music, and is a
hit with a mannered local
and foreign crowd.
✉ **Platnéřská 9**
☎ **24 81 38 92**
Ⓜ **Staroměstská**
🕘 11am-midnight Ⓥ

Country Life (7, E5) **$**
Vegetarian
Highly popular serve-
yourself vegetarian food

Wake up and smell the coffee at the Ebel Coffee House

hall connected to the health food shop of the same name, with a menu of hot meals and salads. The ultra-healthy nondairy food is charged according to weight (19Kč/100g, soups 15Kč). There are also desserts and bakery fare.
✉ **Melantrichova 15**
☎ **24 21 33 66**
Ⓜ **Můstek** ◷ Mon-Thurs 9am-8.30pm, Fri 9am-6pm, Sun 11am-8.30pm ♿ **V**

Ebel Coffee House
(7, B7)   **$**
Cafe
Contender for the best coffee house in Prague, with its numerous custom blends, croissants, bagels and friendly service. The 'express breakfast' (a bagel, latte or double espresso, and juice) is served daily 9am-10pm for 75Kč. It's a relaxing, unpretentious spot that concentrates on making great wake-up coffee.
✉ **Týn Court 2**
☎ **24 89 57 88**
Ⓜ **Náměstí Republiky**
◷ 9am-10pm

Francouzská Restaurace
(7, C10)   **$$$$**
Modern Czech, French
Flashy restaurant in Municipal House, filled with the same gorgeous Art

Nouveau style that permeates the rest of the building. This means that while you're enjoying your cream of Canadian lobster (bisque d'homard), marinated white duck liver, or grilled sea dog, there are at least 10 curious tourists bottlenecking the front entrance.
✉ **Municipal House, náměstí Republiky 5**
☎ **22 00 27 70**
Ⓜ **Náměstí Republiky**
◷ noon-4pm & 6-11pm

Jalapeños (7, B2)   **$$**
Tex-Mex
The mock-adobe 'n' thatchwork interior makes you want to run for a poncho, but you'll soon appreciate the bright airiness of the place. It serves Mexican standards like tacos, burritos and nachos with little fuss. Specialities of the house favour beefsteak.
✉ **Valentinská 8**
☎ **231 29 25**
Ⓜ **Staroměstská**
◷ Mon-Fri 10.30am-11.30pm, Sat-Sun 11am-11.30pm ♿

Klub Architecktů
(3, G6)   **$$**
Modern Czech
Subterranean, stone-walled hideaway with low-slung lighting, perfect for plotting your next corporate raid. Offers a mix of local and international dishes, with

celery pancakes and vegie sausages for vegetarians, and lots of chicken (breaded, baked, roasted and mixed) for the meaty. Service can be dismissive.
✉ **Betlémské náměstí 5**
☎ **24 40 12 14**
Ⓜ **Národní třída**
◷ 11.30am-11.30pm **V**

Kolkovna (3, C7)   **$$**
Traditional Czech
A Pilsener Urquell pub in a triangular block of striking apartment buildings, with lots of beer-friendly dishes like pork pie and fried Olomouc cheese, and Czech regulars like goulash. Cosy, but unforgivably guilty of playing Boney M.
✉ **V Kolkovně 8**
☎ **24 81 97 01**
Ⓜ **Staroměstská**
◷ 11am-midnight

Le Saint-Jacques
(7, B8)   **$$$**
French
Simply elegant family-run French restaurant specialising in all the basic food groups: fish, duck, beef, veal and lamb. Be serenaded by a piano and violin over a candle-lit dinner while imbibing some French wines and enjoying flavoursome home-style cooking.
✉ **Jakubská 4**
☎ **232 26 85**
Ⓜ **Náměstí Republiky**
◷ Mon-Fri 11am-3pm & 6pm-midnight, Sat 6pm-midnight

Lotos (7, C2)   **$**
Vegetarian
Lotos specialises in vegetarian, vegan and macrobiotic meals, and in making you feel relaxed in its sparse environment. It has delicious soups and salads, and specialities like Asian-style tempeh, moussaka

and Serbian risotto. It's also that Prague rarity – a nonsmoking eatery.

✉ Platnéřská 13
☎ 232 23 90
Ⓜ Staroměstská
🕐 noon-10pm ♿ Ⓥ

Mama Lucy (7, B6) $$
Tex-Mex
Attempts the standard new-millennium style mishmash, in this case a single *LIFE* poster, bus-stop benches and a giant jalapeno on the ceiling. It sort of works, but more importantly the food portions are huge and extremely tasty, and the service very attentive.

✉ Dlouhá 2 ☎ 232 72 07 Ⓜ Staroměstská
🕐 11am-midnight

Mikulka's Pizzeria (7, A6) $
Italian
This no-nonsense pizzeria also serves pasta. Vegetarians should read the menu carefully as some vego-style pizzas have meat ('pizza with spinach' also has smoked meat and sausage); it's best to construct your own (from 126Kč).

✉ Dlouhá 8
☎ 231 00 18
Ⓜ Staroměstská
🕐 11am-11.30pm ♿ Ⓥ

Pivnice Radegast (7, C9) $
Beer Hall
Loquacious locals wander the aisles in this busy beer hall. The social atmosphere is enlivening and the nourishment (both solid and liquid) is ridiculously cheap, but the pre-prepared goulash could be better.

✉ Templová 2
☎ 232 82 37
Ⓜ Náměstí Republiky
🕐 11am-12.30am

Rasoi (3, C8) $$$
Indian
Waiters in full cultural regalia, separate tandoori ovens for vegie and meaty meals, and a range of vindaloos – from the warmth-spreading to the fiery – are some of Rasoi's hallmarks. If the enjoyment gets too much for you, retreat to the terrace garden for a hit of hookah (100Kč).

✉ Dlouhá 13 ☎ 232 84 00 Ⓜ Náměstí Republiky 🕐 11.30am-11.30pm ♿ Ⓥ

Restaurace U Betlémské kaple (3, G5) $$
Seafood & Czech
There are plenty of Czech-style sea critters on offer in

this local tavern lined with carved wooden benches. Try the 'drunken catfish' or the well-prepared carp, or sample the fried frogs' thighs. Other Czech specialities like sirloin in cream with dumplings are also available. There's also friendly, attentive service.

✉ Betlémské náměstí 2 ☎ 22 22 16 39 Ⓜ Národní třída
🕐 11am-11pm ♿

Restaurace U medvídků (3, H6) $
Beer Hall
Former brewery with regular big crowds of Czechs and visitors throwing down the cheap beer, venison goulash and dumplings, fried cheese, or the 'beer meals' served after 3pm: beer cheese, herring and liverwurst. Extra oomph (or oompah) delivered by a jovial folk band.

✉ Na Perštýně 7
☎ 24 21 19 16
Ⓜ Národní třída
🕐 11.30am-11pm

Reykjavík (7, E2) $$$-$$$$
Seafood
Go Björk over Icelandic salted cod *(baccala)* in this excellent seafood restaurant disguised as a posh hotel brasserie. Also served is blue fin, eel and three kinds of salted herring. The house speciality cheesecake is fabulous. Light jazz combos practise at dinnertime.

✉ Karlova 20
☎ 22 22 12 18
Ⓜ Staroměstská
🕐 11am-midnight

Rybí trh (7, B7) $$$-$$$$
Seafood
One of Prague's most accomplished seafood

Going Green

Vegetarian food in Prague ranges from pure, lovingly prepared dishes (**Lotos**; p. 79) to food so confidently titled it sounds like the latest fashion accessory (**Radost FX Cafe**; p. 82) to some pretty poor imitations. Dedicated vegetarian restaurants are quite rare in the inner city.

Be wary of places that appear in generic 'Vegetarian' listings in tourist leaflets – quite often they exaggerate to get the trade. Except in authentic vegetarian places, check the ingredients in the dishes, as it's not uncommon for your potential vegie meal to include fish, or in some cases a fistful of ham.

restaurants, 'Fish Market', lives up to its name by acquiring fresh catches daily (see the mound of ice inside) and preparing it how you like it. Specialities include sushi, and lobster plucked from the internal aquarium. Conveniently, the owners also run the excellent wine shop next door.

✉ **Týn Court 5**
☎ 24 89 54 47
Ⓜ **Náměstí Republiky**
🕐 11am-midnight

Richard Nebeský

The seafood at Rybí trh is right off the scales.

Safir Grill (7, F5) $
Middle Eastern
Wolf down some felafel or shish kebab at the small counter or a table in the back. Fast and efficient, this place also serves up *smažený sýv* (fried cheese) and vegetarian interpretations of its specialities (still not sure what to make of the menu item called 'vegetarian eggplant' though).

✉ **Havelská 12**
☎ 24 22 11 43
Ⓜ **Můstek** 🕐 Mon-Sat 10am-8pm ♿ **V**

Sarah Bernhardt
(7, B10) $$$$
French, Modern Czech
They don't come much grander than this, an Art Nouveau feast for the eyes and a French/Czech banquet for the stomach. The menu is enough to make those of us who haven't tried Azerbaijani caviar weep, though we're less tempted by Mucha's alleged favourite dish: stuffed backside of rabbit.

✉ **Hotel Paříž, U Obecního domu 1**
☎ 22 19 51 95
Ⓜ **Náměstí Republiky**
🕐 noon-4pm & 6pm-midnight

Siam-I-San
(7, B2) $$$
Thai, Vegetarian
You'll find the delicious gamut of authentic Thai cuisine in this top-notch restaurant, from *nuer sa wan* (pan-fried marinated beef) to *kra prao koong* (stir-fried prawns with chilli and assorted vegetables). The unique crockery, cutlery and glasses can be bought in the adjoining Arzenal.

✉ **Valentinská 11**
☎ 24 81 40 99
Ⓜ **Staroměstská**
🕐 10am-midnight **V**

Staroměstská restaurace
(7, C6) $$-$$$
Modern Czech
This sprawling Old Town Square tourist eatery serves up dependable regional offerings like goulash and a Moravian wedding plate (cabbage, bacon & potato dumplings). If hungry, order a whole duck for 600Kč, or jack up your cholesterol with cream-and-strawberry-stuffed crepes. Be warned that eating and drinking on the terrace will cost you up to 60% more than inside.

✉ **Staroměstské náměstí 5**
☎ 24 21 30 15
Ⓜ **Můstek**
🕐 9am-midnight ♿

Století (3, G4) $-$$
Traditional Czech
Století (Century) backs up its age-themed name by serving bygone celebrities on a plate. Ordering 'Max Dvořák' will net you a vegetable salad with meatballs, 'Ernest Hemingway' is grilled beefsteak flambéed in gin, and 'Marlene Dietrich' is stuffed avocado with whipped Roquefort and marzipan. Gimmicks aside, this place is sincerely good value.

✉ **Karolíny Světlé 21**
☎ 22 22 00 08
Ⓜ **Národní třída**
🕐 noon-midnight **V**

Toscana (7, E4) $$$
Italian
There are two Toscana's, one a shamefully touristy pizzeria off Malé náměstí, the other a shamefully indulgent dining experience among embroidered linen, cast-iron chairs, piano music and lots of mellow lights. Service can be aloof and they like Barry White, but the vineyard-sized wine list and authentic Italian cuisine balance it out.

✉ **Michalská 22-23**
☎ 21 61 15 36
Ⓜ **Staroměstská**
🕐 11am-11pm

Týnská Literary Cafe
(7, B7) $
Cafe
Publisher-run cafe where all the decoration has been removed to allow literary ideas to bounce unrestricted around the interior and the busy courtyard. The only obstructions are assorted literary magazines, lots of tables, and a basket of sweet rolls (this is not a cafe for foodies). There are also readings.
✉ Týnská 6
☎ 24 82 78 07
Ⓜ Náměstí Republiky
🕐 Mon-Fri 9am-11pm, Sat-Sun 10am-11pm

U provaznice
(7, F7) $$
Beer Hall
Appealingly straightforward pub, popular with locals and in a fairly untrammelled side-street. Trades off a myth involving a rope-maker's wife who gets murdered by her hubby, which is supposed to encourage you to touch her portrait for romantic luck (because she had so much of it, right?) and then down lots of beer celebrate.
✉ Provaznická 3
☎ 24 23 25 28
Ⓜ Muzeum 🕐 11am-midnight

U zlatého tygra
(7, E3) $
Beer Hall
Bill Clinton apparently gets escorted here by Havel every time he visits the capital. If so, he's one of the few foreigners who actually manages to get a seat at this perpetually full, raucous local's pub. Make sure you get here bright and early if you want to be surrounded by old-timers talking loudly over endless glasses of beer.
✉ Husova 17 ☎ 22 22 11 11 Ⓜ Staroměstská
🕐 3-11pm

VINOHRADY

Ambiente (6, B5) $$
Tex-Mex, Italian
Catering to the local business crowd, it has a bright atmosphere and good basic steaks, burritos and pastas. Disappointingly, they advertise 'cocktails for sweet ladies', but no 'booze for butch blokes'.
✉ Mánesova 59
☎ 627 59 13 Ⓜ Náměstí Míru 🕐 Mon-Fri 11am-midnight, Sat-Sun 4pm-midnight

Kavárna Medúza
(6, E2) $
Cafe
Subdued conversation abounds in this spontaneously decorated cafe. Favoured by a low-key younger clientele, it's away from the maddening crowd.
✉ Belgická 17 ☎ 22 51 51 07 Ⓜ Náměstí Míru 🕐 Mon-Fri 11am-1am, Sat-Sun noon-1am

Kojak's (6, B3) $$
Tex-Mex
Have a lollipop, or maybe

just one of the meaty specials like 'cajun piggy' in this tenuous culinary tribute to the bald-headed avenger.
✉ Anny Letenské 16
☎ 22 25 05 94
Ⓜ Náměstí Míru
🕐 Mon-Fri 11.30am-midnight, Sat-Sun 3pm-midnight ♿

Modrá řeka (6, A2) $$
Yugoslavian
The simple, homely 'Blue River' will lull you into a good mood with its sunny walls and exceptional homemade cooking. Try *urnebes* (spicy cheese spread), the mince meat-filled peppers, or something from the long list of vegie choices.
✉ Mánesova 13
☎ 22 25 16 01
Ⓜ Náměstí Míru
🕐 Mon-Fri 11am-11pm, Sat-Sun 5-11pm Ⓥ

Ponte (6, B1) $$-$$$
Modern Czech
Set in the middle of some busy Vinohrady acreage,

Ponte proves it's wise to international cuisine by combining such disparate foods as pork and eggplant and making them taste good together, and at a reasonable upmarket price.
✉ Anglická 15
☎ 24 22 16 55
Ⓜ Náměstí Míru
🕐 11.30am-midnight

Radost FX Cafe
(6, C1) $-$$
Vegetarian
Part of the uber-glamorous Radost entertainment complex, this vegetarian cafe was created to give the impression that hitting a club until early morning is part of every healthy lifestyle. It's not, so embrace your vices and then enjoy some of the most innovative food around, from spinach burgers to pesto-stuffed ravioli.
✉ Bělehradská 120
☎ 24 25 47 76
Ⓜ IP Pavlova 🕐 Mon-Fri 11.30am-5am, Sat-Sun 5pm-5am ♿ Ⓥ

WORTH A TRIP

Černý kohout
(4, K3) $$$
Traditional Czech
Unfortunately, you'll need a car to reach Černý kohout (Black Rooster) in the south-western district of Jinonice, but this restaurant has a great reputation for stylish surroundings and traditional Czech food like roast boar. Don't bother bringing a credit card, though, because they don't take 'em.
✉ **Bublavska 308**
☎ 51 68 11 91
🚖 take a taxi
🕐 Mon-Fri 11am-10pm, Sat-Sun 11am-11pm

Corso (4, C8) $-$$
Italian, Traditional Czech
Though Corso has more ceiling decorations and painted glass than many churches, its menu is all straightforward pasta dishes and good traditional Czech cooking, from goulash to roasted pork-knee. It also has a remarkably large fish in a remarkably tiny tank; don't try and stare it down because you'll lose, trust me.
✉ **Dukelských Hrdinů 48**
☎ 80 65 41
Ⓜ Vltavská
🕐 11am-midnight

Hong Kong (4, C8) $$
Chinese
A huge menu, big servings, separate smoking and nonsmoking areas, and good Chinese food are reasons why you should drop in for lunch or dinner if you're in the Bubeneč/Holešovice area. Staff even have the compassion to turn the Canto-pop down to a bearable level.
✉ **Letenské náměstí 5**
☎ 33 37 62 09
Ⓜ Hradčanská, then tram 1, 8, 25, 26, 51 or 56 to Letenské náměstí 🕐 11am-3pm & 6-11pm

Huang He (4, G9) $$
Chinese
You'll soon discover that Huang He has built up some hefty credentials as a local favourite. Apparently, it's well worth the pilgrimage into the suburbs for those who appreciate excellent Chinese at very good prices.
✉ **Vršovická 1**
☎ 71 74 66 51
🚖 take a taxi
🕐 11am-11pm ♿

Restaurant u Cedru
(4, C5) $$
Lebanese
Spot the regulars, who usually huddle in the corners, in this friendly fooderie. You're likely to find that it's a thoroughly annoying place to visit because there are simply too many good things on the menu to cram into your mouth in one sitting. You can get 10 of your Lebanese favourites (stuffed vine leaves, pickles, spinach pastry etc) for around 775Kč.
✉ **Na Hutích 13**
☎ 33 34 29 74
Ⓜ Dejvická
🕐 11am-11pm Ⓥ

Stuff to Savour
Try these places to pump up your sugar levels or to take a break from the taste of goulash and dumplings. **Cream & Dream** (Husova 12; 7, E3; ☎ 24 21 10 35) has lots of exotically swirled, fruity Italian ice creams, while out back is a bar well stocked with Moravian wine, spirits and liqueurs. **Odkolek** (Rytířská 12; 3, G7) is part of a bakery chain, and does a roaring trade most days. Towards Josefov, **Paneria** (Kaprova; 3, D5; ☎ 35 36 44 63) has tarts, snails (the pastry kind), and filled croissants and baguettes.

At **Michelské pekařství** (Dušní 1; 7, A6; ☎ 22 31 65 16) you'll find pretzels, eclairs, tarts and open rolls/baguettes. **Gourmand au Gourmand** (Dlouhá 10; 7, A6; ☎ 232 90 60) has luscious tarts, cakes and pies, and some of the best Italian ice cream around.

entertainment

The history of this striking old city can't help playing a part in the exuberant local entertainment scene, be it providing a grand auditorium like Smetana Hall or several dozen churches in which to stage familiar and newly discovered operas, drama and classical concerts, or the atmospheric stone cellar of a centuries-old building in which Czech musicians blaze away on guitars, saxophones and vocal cords. There are plenty of more contemporary venues too, with some ultra-modern clubs, lots of suave bars and refreshingly down-to-earth pubs just waiting to be stumbled through.

There are plenty of places to jazz up a trip to Prague.

Although there are places with almost exclusively Czech patronage and a fair few that resound with more foreign accents than Robin Williams on speed, most central hangouts attract a mixed bunch. The same goes for where the entertainment hangs out, with no single area claiming all the best spots. Staré Město is riddled with theatres, bars and live-music joints, with some of the flashier ones crowded around Pařížská and in the maze of streets behind Týn Church – many good jazz spots lie between Old Town Square and Národní. Clubs are strewn from Smíchov to Holešovice and everywhere in-between, including the busy Malostranské náměstí. The industrial landscape of Žižkov is home to some arty cinemas, experimental performance venues, and gay clubs – the gay scene isn't concentrated in one district but rather is spread around the inner city. The area south of the National Theatre to Myslíková is one of the freshest, hippest zones, with a lot of young clubs, bars and cafes opening up there.

The imposing symbol of Czech culture, the Prague National Theatre

Richard Nebesky

There are many publications with entertainment details: what's on, where, and what it's like. The 'Night & Day' section of the weekly *Prague Post* is good for basically everything. *Czech Culture* is a fine monthly with details of galleries, theatres, music spots and cinemas; the same goes for the Czech-language *Prehled*. *Houser* is a Czech-language booklet that is slanted to hip youth, while *Do města Downtown* is a free bi-monthly leaflet for film, clubbing and the theatre. *Amigo* magazine thoroughly covers gay entertainment.

SPECIAL EVENTS

January *Febiofest* – 25-31 January; International Festival of Film, Television & Video prompts screenings of new international films across the Czech Republic

March *AghaRTA Prague Jazz Festival* – until December; top-drawer jazz artists and orchestras play at AghaRTA and elsewhere in the city

April *Musica Ecumenica* – 7-16 April; International Festival of Spiritual Music, in various ethereal venues around town

Burning of the Witches (Pálení čarodějnic) – 30 April; not literally, just the traditional burning of brooms to ward off evil, accompanied by lots of backyard end-of-winter bonfires

Musica Sacra Praga – Easter, August, October; the Festival of Sacred Music takes place in a number of churches and concert halls, presenting material by Brahms, Puccini and Dvořák among others

May *Majáles* – 1 May; student-celebrated spring festival with a parade from Jana Palacha to Old Town Square

Festival of Chamber Music – 3 May to 3 June; tribute to Czech composers and Mozart at Bertramka, site of a Mozart Museum in Smíchov

Prague Spring (Pražské jaro) International Music Festival – 12 May to 4 June; the most prestigious classical music event in Prague takes place at various concert halls, churches and theatres

June *ET Jam* – rock and alternative music gig at Autokemp Džbán camp site in Vokovice

Dance Prague (Tanec Praha) – 9-28 June; International Festival of Modern Dance, with innovative performances at venues like the Archa Theatre

Ethnic Festival – 17 June to 23 September; folklore performed at the Municipal Library theatre by traditionally costumed Czech and Slovakian ensembles

August *Verdi Festival* – to September; nothing but Verdi operas at the Prague State Opera

September *Burčak* – sweet, cider-like liquid syphoned off at the initial stage of fermentation of new grape crops, and available for only a few weeks every year

Mozart Iuventus – 4-29 September; Mozart Festival at Bertramka featuring young artists playing his tunes, plus compositions written for the occasion

Prague Autumn – 12 September to 3 October; same concept as the more esteemed Prague Spring International Music Festival, but in autumn

Svatováclavské slavnosti – 16-28 September; St Wenceslas Festival of spiritual art, encompassing music, painting and sculpture

October *International Jazz Festival* – 24-27 October; traditional jazz at popular haunts like Lucerna Music Bar and Reduta

November *Musica Iudaica* – Festival of Jewish Music, focusing on the composers of Terezín

December *Festival Bohuslava Martinů (Bohuslav Martinů Music Festival)* – 7-13 December; classical music festival dedicated to a famous Czech composer of the 20th century

BARS & PUBS

Alcohol Bar (7, A5)
The superb selection of booze at this aptly named drinker's shrine includes 250 types of whisky – a statistic to sober an alcoholic and force a teetotaller onto a liquid diet. It's spacious, so you don't have to worry about tottering into fellow connoisseurs, and it has a well-stocked humidor. Gets going late.
✉ **Dušní 6, Staré Město** ☎ **24 81 17 44** Ⓜ **Staroměstská** ◷ **7pm-3am**

Banana Café (7, C8)
Recently anointed A-list hangout, so eclectically cluttered you can't actually see it. Social mountaineers come here to munch on tapas and popcorn, and groove in their collectively ironic way to allegedly chic entertainment like electric boogie. Freshly shucked oysters available out front.
✉ **Štupartská 9, Staré Město** ☎ **57 53 50 50** @ **info@laprovence.cz; www.laprovence.cz** Ⓜ **Náměstí Republiky** ◷ **10pm-3am**

Barfly (3, G5)
Snug cellar spot with a mellow candle-lit interior, good for a romantic rendezvous, quiet conversation, or, for that matter, a relaxed descent into intoxication. The bar meals are sizeable and tasty – try the excellent risotto.
✉ **U Dobřenských 3, Staré Město** ☎ **22 22 21 41** Ⓜ **Národní třída** ◷ **Mon noon-1am, Tues-Thurs noon-2am, Fri-Sun noon-3am**

Blue Light (2, D5)
Ostensibly a jazz cavern, but its boisterous gigs had been suspended at the time of writing (hopefully only temporarily) due to a run-in with a flashing blue light over noise levels. Regardless, this is still a great place for a drink amid old jazz posters, graffiti-traced walls, and lungfuls of smoke.
✉ **Josefská 1, Malá Strana** ☎ **57 53 31 26** Ⓜ **Malostranská** ◷ **6pm-3am**

Bugsy's Bar (7, A4)
Technically on Kostečná, this deluxe-diner look-a-like is an upmarket crowd favourite due to the panache with which it pours American-style cocktails down their throats.

Making her mark at the Blue Light Jazz Club

Mixes a deliciously mean Manhattan. Suspenders *de rigueur* for the bar staff, who wade professionally among the Art Deco standing tables and padded booths.
✉ **Pařížská 10, Staré Město** ☎ **232 99 43** @ **www.bugsysbar.com** Ⓜ **Staroměstská** ◷ **7pm-2am, live Cuban music Mon from 9pm**

Café Montmartre
(7, E3) It will ultimately take more than a couch with broken springs, a ceiling fresco and a hat-stand to live up to the aesthetic standard of an artist-riddled Parisian district, but this cafe is still a worthy place for a relaxing vino, brew, or cuppa.
✉ **Retězová 7, Staré Město** ☎ **22 22 12 44** Ⓜ **Staroměstská** ◷ **Mon-Fri 9am-11pm, Sat-Sun noon-11pm**

Česká vinotéka
(3, B8) Corridor-sized wine bar serving only Czech *bílé* (white) and *červené* (red) wines. No room for tour

The A-list goes bananas for this icy-cool cafe.

Richard Nebesky

Getting into Top Beer

Pivo means beer and it's one of the most frequently uttered (though not always intelligible) words in a republic whose citizens distinguish themselves by being the biggest consumers of beer in the world, downing on average 160L per person each year. The most popular of the many fine and inexpensive local brews are Pilsener Urquell and Gambrinus. Other brands include Staropramen and Budvar (the original and better Budweiser), plus the output of many excellent microbreweries.

The 10, 12 or other numeral designated to beers along with a degree symbol thankfully doesn't represent alcohol content. It's a measurement of the density of the pre-fermentation beer mixture – 10° beers are dark beers, while 12° are generally lighter.

---

groups here, just locals, and local vintages for around 30-40Kč per glass. If you prefer the anaemic-style of grape, try the delicious Rulandské bílé (Pinot Blanc). Regional cheeses and smoked meats are available out the back.
✉ Anežská 3, Josefov
☎ 22 31 12 93
Ⓜ Náměstí Republiky
◷ Mon-Fri 1pm-midnight, Sat 2-10pm

Chateau (7, B8)
The only thing that's changed since this place was called 'Chapeau' is one consonant: it's retained the frat boys, witching-hour ambience, and iron-on cool. Everything in this bar is backlit, including the smiles of the clientele; black T-shirt compulsory.
✉ Jakubská 2, Staré Město ☎ 22 31 63 28
e www.czrb.cz
Ⓜ Náměstí Republiky
◷ noon-5am

James Joyce (7, F2)
Picture a roomful of people quietly sipping port, nibbling quail eggs and discussing passages recently

browsed in their dog-eared copies of *Ulysses*. This James Joyce does not exist. The one that does is an often-raucous Irish pub where Guinness is downed along with cheddar and mustard mash, and where football is highbrow.
✉ Liliová 10, Staré Město ☎ 24 24 87 93
e joyce.bary@mail.a-z prague.cz Ⓜ Staroměstská ◷ 10.30am-12.30am

Jo's Bar (2, E4)
Longstanding favourite of backpackers, who crowd the front booths to wolf down burgers and watch screen-projected episodes of *The Simpsons*; the alcoves out the back are generally quieter (though not by much). Those of you prone to over-festiveness take note of the sign on the door: 'No outside screaming, being after 10pm'.
✉ Malostranské náměstí 7, Malá Strana ☎ 0602 971 478
e www.jos-bar.com
Ⓜ Malostranská
◷ 11am-late

Konvikt Pub (3, G6)
Good honest pub populated by refreshed locals and the odd tourist taking a well-earned gulp between classical concerts. Avoids the raucousness of similar places and serves cheap and tasty Czech meals.
✉ Bartolomějská 11, Staré Město ☎ 24 23 24 27 Ⓜ Národní třída
◷ noon-1am

Marquis de Sade
(7, B8) High-ceilinged den of liquidity, where absinthe is thrown back among decrepit red-velour couches, scruffy saloon tables, and sinfully large artwork. The building was a brothel in a previous life, hence the small 'viewing' balcony upstairs; nowadays it's the bar staff who look after the demanding clientele.
✉ Templová 8, Staré Město ☎ 24 81 75 05
e marquis.bary@ mail.a-zprague.cz
Ⓜ Náměstí Republiky
◷ 11am-2am

O'Che's (7, E2)
The only revolutionary spirits you'll find in this

Come the revolution, O'Che's will have the decor right.

Richard Nebeský

whimsical tavern are on the shelves behind the paraphernalia-riddled bar. Caters to sports-starved drinkers who need a dose of football or rugby with their Guinness, and dishes out decent (though pricey) blackboard specials to soak up your tipple.

✉ **Liliová 14, Staré Město** ☎ 22 22 11 78 **e** oches@volny.cz; www.oches.com **Ⓜ** Staroměstská ☺ 10am-1am

Pivnice U černého vola (5, C3)

Diminutive pub with a gaily decorated facade and a constant stream of Czech drinkers heaving themselves on/off benches all day; either that or they've paid two-dozen guys to do a continuous loop through the bar, around the Loreta and back. Stand-up beer 'bar' in the front entrance is good for a quick thirst-quencher.

✉ **Loretánské náměstí 1, Hradčany Ⓜ** Malostranská, then tram 22 or 23 to Pohořelec ☺ 10am-10pm

Pivovarský Dům

(4, F7) Microbrewery/ restaurace popular with Czech drinkers of all ages. Interior has a bit of Art Nouveau swish and old brewery artefacts decorate the windows. But it's the speciality beers that people come here for, namely classic pale and dark lagers, the surprisingly tasty champagne beer, banana beer and sour cherry beer.

✉ **Lípová 15 (entry on Ječná), Nové Město** ☎ 96 21 66 66 **e** www.gastroinfo.cz/ pivodum **Ⓜ** IP Pavlova ☺ 11am-11.30pm

Propaganda (3, J5)

This impressively busy neighbourhood joint gets so full there's little need for nonhuman decoration, so it makes do with ceiling gauze, a few photos, and a football-table out the back that you'll have to fight to get on. Unpretentious except for the homespun propaganda on the placemats.

✉ **Pštrossova 29, Nové Město** ☎ 0602 97 50 83 **e** www.volny.cz/ propagandabar **Ⓜ** Národní třída ☺ Mon-Fri 3pm-2am, Sat-Sun 5pm-2am

Sektbar Pontoon

(3, D4) Despite its generally scuffed appearance, this waterlogged bar is actually

a pretty good place to sit and gaze out across the slow-flowing Vltava to the grand silhouette of Prague Castle. It's obviously best in summer, but on a cooler, less-crowded afternoon it can feel like you have the river to yourself.

✉ **beside Mánesův most, Staré Město** ☎ 231 99 52 **Ⓜ** Staroměstská ☺ 10am-dusk

Vinotéka U Zlatého Hada (2, F5)

Cosy, slouch-worthy wine bar with a superb range of Moravian and other Czechfermented drops, along with some imported bottles. You can fortify your fuzzy mood with spirits or cigars, or banish it with a cup of Jamaica Blue Mountain káva.

✉ **Maltézské náměstí 3, Malá Strana** ☎ 57 53 14 72 **e** www.zlatyhad.cz **Ⓜ** Malostranská ☺ Mon-Fri 10am-9pm, Sat-Sun 2-9pm

Zoo Bar (7, E4)

Could be just another cellar-dwelling bar frequented by a mixture of local and foreign enthusiasts, but there's something extra appealing about the elbow-polished bar and the table-crowded cavern further within – it's a great place for the evening's first drink. Note that it lacks signage, except for a scrawl on the open front doors. Low-key shows feature jazz, blues, acoustic or rock.

✉ **Jilská 18, Staré Město e** zoonews@ hotmail.com **Ⓜ** Můstek ☺ 5pm-1am, music Fri-Sat 9.30pm **⑤** shows 40-50Kč

CLUBS

Futurum (4, F6)
Has record launches, alternative bands and various DJs in attendance but mostly it's a case of back to the future – the 'future' being when hairdos resembled explosions (1980s) and alternative music started sounding just like mainstream music (1990s). If you're nostalgic for either, this is your place.
✉ **Zborovská 7, Smíchov**
☎ **57 32 85 71**
e **www.musicbar .cz/futurum/index/htm**
Ⓜ **Anděl** ⏱ **8am-3am, box office from 7pm, shows 9pm**
Ⓢ **80-130Kč**

Garáž (2, E4)
Spirited two-level bar/club down the spiral staircase at Jo's, usually well-patronised by chatter-hungry expats and backpackers until the wee hours, with a peak in attendance during a Happy Hour that's been time-warped to last from 6-10pm. Impossibly, the lower level is even darker than the one above.
✉ **Malostranské náměstí 7, Malá Strana**
☎ **0602 971 478**
Ⓜ **Malostranská**
⏱ **6pm-late, Wed-Sat DJs from 9pm** Ⓢ **free**

Karlovy Lázně (3, F4)
Four-level designer concrete bunker accommodating hundreds of teeny shuffling feet. You can watch live bands at ground level (MCM Café), boogie on 1 (Discothéque), mime *Holiday* and other late 20th-century ditties on 2 (Kaleidoskop), or bypass them all and head for the solid drum'n'bass and break beat on 3 (Paradogs).
✉ **Novotného lávka, Staré Město** ☎ **22 22 05 02** **e** **www.karlovy lazne.cz** Ⓜ **Staroměstská** ⏱ **9pm-5am** Ⓢ **50-100Kč**

Mecca (4, C9)
Walking into this ultra-fashionable, designer-person hangout is like walking into the *Jetsons* living room – all stark colours, space-age vinyl couches, and the sorts of chairs that challenge you to try and sit on them. Fashion people, ad-folk and architects flock to Mecca's industrial-chic club to dance sweatlessly to house, drum'n'bass and techno.
✉ **U Průhonu, Holešovice** ☎ **83 87 05 22** **e** **mecca@mecca .cz; www.mecca.cz**
Ⓜ **Nádraží Holešovice**
⏱ **Mon-Thurs 11am-11pm, Fri-Sat 11am-6am (club from 10pm)**
Ⓢ **150-250Kč**

Radost FX (6, C1)
If beauty is only skin-deep, then Radost revels unapologetically in shallowness. Its bohemian lounge is appealingly decked out in mosaic-topped tables and sumptuous chaises longues, while the downstairs club has leopard-print benches and

Absinthe Makes the Heart Grow Fonder

Actually, absinthe rots the brain thanks to its wormwood flavouring, or at least this was the consensus that led to the banning of the powerful green spirit (70% alcohol content) across Europe in the early 20th century after many years of vigorous consumption, particularly in France. As is the case in times of prohibition, though, this often just increased the forbidden appeal of absinthe (*absinth* in Czech), particularly to literate drunks like Ernest Hemingway.

The concoction was outlawed in Czechoslovakia during the Communist era, but was legalised again in the 1990s after being re-adopted by Czech trendsetters, who strangely believed that acquiring an epic hangover gave them anti-establishment kudos.

lava-lamp spotlights. Join the handsome, terminally languid crowd in grooving to hip hop, house and funk sounds from top-notch DJs.
- ✉ **Bělehradská 120, Vinohrady**
- ☎ **24 25 47 76**
- e **www.radostfx.cz**
- Ⓜ **IP Pavlova**
- ◷ **lounge Wed-Sun 11am-5am, club Wed-Sun 10pm-5am**
- Ⓢ **100-250Kč**

Roxy (3, C9)
The expansive floor of this iconic, ramshackle old theatre has seen many a hard-edged DJ and band over the years, plus plenty of experimental fare in the form of drama, dance and short films. All shadowy nooks and crannies usually fill up quickly once the doors open, even the stairwell boudoirs.
- ✉ **Dlouhá 33, Josefov**
- ☎ **24 82 62 96**
- e **roxy@roxy.cz; www.roxy.cz**
- Ⓜ **Náměstí Republiky**
- ◷ **8pm-late**
- Ⓢ **50-350Kč (Mon free)**

Solidní nejistota
(3, K5) Wildly popular with an older Czech crowd, Solidní nejistota (which confusingly translates as 'Solid Uncertainty') has a vaguely medieval torture-chamber feel due to the blood-red interior and cast-iron fittings; the torture theme is accentuated by the choice of 1980s disco to enliven the microscopic dance floor. The huge stone bar is highly conducive to a slow drink.
- ✉ **Pštrossova 21, Nové Město** ☎ **24 91 05 93**

- Ⓜ **Národní třída**
- ◷ **Mon-Fri noon-3am, Sat-Sun 6pm-6am**
- Ⓢ **free**

Tendr (7, B5)
Pretty much every night at this enthusiastic, by-the-numbers Latin club is S&M night: 'salsa & meringue', that is. The unintimidating surrounds and a few selections from the swollen cocktail menu might inspire you to let one of their dance instructors show you the authentic way to fall over your feet.
- ✉ **Pařížská 6, Staré Město** ☎ **24 81 36 05**
- e **juan@salsa.cz**
- Ⓜ **Staroměstská**
- ◷ **6pm-5am**
- Ⓢ **Fri-Sat from 9pm 100Kč, Sun-Thurs from 9pm 50Kč**

JAZZ

AghaRTA Jazz Centrum (3, K10)
This venerable, decade-old club, named after a Miles Davis recording, stages top-quality modern Czech jazz in its humbly furnished auditorium. Don't worry if you turn up and no one else is there – the bulk of the audience usually barges in about 30mins before showtime. Check out the

AghaRTA Jazz Centrum... and all that jazz

Richard Nebeský

CD counter (see p. 63) for some great jazz buys.
- ✉ **Krakovská 5, Nové Město** ☎ **22 21 12 75**
- e **2hp@arta.cz; www.agharta.cz**
- Ⓜ **Muzeum** ◷ **bar & shop 7pm-midnight, shows 9pm-midnight**
- Ⓢ **100Kč**

Jazz Boat (3, B6)
This vessel's 2.5hr Vltava-cruising concerts are pitched forcefully at tourists, but some popular local musos perform here. Its 'restaurant' offers unremarkable food and beverage at steepish extra cost.
- ✉ **EVD pier No 5, under Čechův most, Josefov**
- ☎ **0603 551 680**
- e **www.jazzboat.cz**
- Ⓜ **Staroměstská**
- ◷ **Tues-Sun 8.30-11pm**
- Ⓢ **590Kč**

Jazz Club Železná
(7, D6) Subterranean venue with a wonderfully innovative program of jazz, rock and blues, and the odd bit of offbeat theatre; also sells secondhand jazz CDs. A mixed crowd of locals and travellers regularly pack it to its stone ceiling. If you hear that Tres Hombres are playing here, don't miss them.
- ✉ **Železná 16, Staré Město** ☎ **24 23 96 97**
- e **info@jazzclub.cz; www.jazzclub.cz**
- Ⓜ **Můstek** ◷ **3pm-12.30am, shows 9pm-midnight** Ⓢ **120Kč**

Metropolitan Jazz Club (3, J8)
Basement jazz'n'blues haunt, with easily digestible ragtime and swing compositions often

Playing Solo

Entertaining your sole self in Prague is easy and uncomplicated. Cafes and bars are invariably dotted with unaccompanied Czechs and foreigners enjoying their own company or the qualities of a good book, newspaper or menu, while live music venues also have their share of self-possessed attendees.

Though wandering into a noisy crowded beer hall on your own may at first appear an intimidating exercise, just head for a space at a less-populated bench and inquire 'Je tu volno' ('Is it free?') before sitting down. You may even find yourself waved over to a spare spot with companionable, refreshment-flowing consequences.

occupying the aural space. There's a preference for substance over style, hence the plain-tiled floor and general lack of adornment that will have interior decorators pulling their catalogues out in frustration.
✉ Jungmannova 14, Nové Město ☎ 24 21 60 25 @ metropolitan@telecom.cz Ⓜ Národní třída ⏰ Mon-Fri 11am-1am, Sat-Sun 7pm-1am, shows 9pm-12.30am
⑤ 100Kč

Reduta (3, H6)
Intimate jazz setting, with well-attired patrons squeezing into tiered seats and lounges to soak up the big-band, swing and dixieland atmosphere. Shares a passageway with Rock Café, a fact the purists who have to pass the rock-ruckus probably don't appreciate. Occasionally oversells tickets, causing a last-minute scramble for seating.
✉ Národní 20, Nové Město ☎ 24 91 22 46 @ www.redutajazzclub.cz Ⓜ Národní třída ⏰ box office Mon-Fri from 3pm, Sat-Sun from 7pm, shows 9pm-midnight ⑤ 280-300Kč

U Malého Glena
(2, E4) Smorgasbord of jazz styles (and blues) served up nightly in this informal venue, including modern, acid and vocal. Jam sessions are regularly held here – people adept at rattling spoons and slapping their knees are in the wrong place, but those who can manage even the odd note are welcome.
✉ Karmelitská 23, Malá Strana
☎ 57 53 17 17
@ www.malyglen.cz
Ⓜ Malostranská
⏰ 10am-2am, shows 9pm ⑤ 100-150Kč

Ungelt Jazz & Blues Club (7, C7)
This popular poky/smoky vault venue can be crammed with people attracted by 'Free Jazz' signage around the Old Town Square, but it appears an admission price is usually charged. Get there early if you decide to brave the crowds, or just hang out in the exuberant Czech-dominated pub upstairs.
✉ Týnská ulička 2, Staré Město
☎ 24 89 57 48

@ www.mobilecritic.com/ungelt.php3
Ⓜ Náměstí Republiky
⏰ pub noon-midnight, jazz club 8pm-late, shows 9pm-midnight
⑤ 200Kč

U Staré Paní (7, F4)
Located in the bowels of the hotel of the same name, this well-established jazz club caters to all levels of musical appreciation. It also delves into Czech-performed blues and rock.
✉ Michalská 9, Staré Město ☎ 24 22 80 90
@ www.ustarepani.cz
Ⓜ Můstek ⏰ 7pm-1am, shows 9pm-midnight ⑤ 160Kč

Richard Nebeský

Catch some one-bar blues at U Staré Paní.

ROCK, BLUES & FOLK

Blues Sklep U krále Jiřího (7, F2)
This stone-walled, slate-floored dugout resounds with blues, jazz and funk chords. Gets a combined crowd of Prague-folk and tourists to watch local notables like the cheerfully haggard Stan the Blues Man.
✉ Liliová 10, Staré Město
☎ 24 24 87 94
e www.kinggeorge.cz
Ⓜ Staroměstská
◷ Mon-Sat 7pm-1am, shows 9pm-midnight
⑤ 60Kč

Dlabačov Hall (4, E4)
The Czech Song and Dance Ensemble, formed in 1947, is the republic's sole professional folk performance troupe, though other 'folklore' events are irregularly and mostly less impressively staged elsewhere by private companies.
✉ Hotel Pyramida, Bělohorská 24, Hradčany
☎ 33 37 34 75
e www.czechfolklore.cz
Ⓜ Hradčanská, then tram 8 to Malovanka
◷ shows Mar-Nov Mon-Sat 8.30pm
⑤ 450Kč

Klub 007 (4, F5)
Inconspicuous location under stairs on the eastern side of dorm block 7, but conspicuously loud punk, death metal, jungle and hip-hop is enjoyed by procrastinating students and aficionados of strong, raw music (and dirt-cheap *pivo*). Where James likes to chill with Moneypenny after assignments.
✉ Block 7, Strahov dormitory complex,
Chaloupekého 7, Strahov ☎ 57 21 14 39
e www.klub007strahov.cz Ⓜ Dejvická, then bus 143, 149 or 217 to Chaloupekého ◷ Mon-Sat 7.30pm-1am, shows 8pm ⑤ 120Kč

La Comedie (7, A8)
Cocktail bar and salsa-crazy club hosting live music, from Russian saxophonists to blues to rock and back again. In the few hours prior to the 'Latino Disco' firing up, there's usually a dance class teaching you how to trip the salsa, meringue and casino fantastic.
✉ Malá Štupartská 5, Staré Město
☎ 24 82 80 49
e www.lacomedie.com
Ⓜ Náměstí Republiky
◷ Mon-Wed noon-2am, Thurs-Sat noon-5am, Sun 3pm-midnight; live music Sun-Thurs 9pm ⑤ free

Lucerna Music Bar (3, H9) Pick your night in this large, endearing old theatre at random and you could end up watching anything from an Arabic jazz orchestra to a Beatles covers band, an '80s disco, or Czech blues, rock or folk. A spontaneously nominated evening netted us the memorably surreal experience of a '50s cabaret show-cum-dancehall.
✉ Lucerna Passage, Vodičkova 36, Nové Město ☎ 24 21 71 08
e www.musicbar.cz
Ⓜ Muzeum ◷ cafe 11am-5pm, bar 8pm-3am, shows 9pm
⑤ 50-150Kč

Malostranská beseda (2, D5) The unpretentious upstairs environs of the former town hall of Malá Strana is now favoured by Czechs of all ages for its nightly agenda of rock, jazz, folk and country (or in this case republic) music performers. Packs out early, particularly on weekends.
✉ Malostranské náměstí 21, Malá Strana

Rockin' on at the Lucerna Bar

☎ 57 53 20 92
📧 www.tulak.cz/
beseda/index.php
Ⓜ Malostranská
🕐 bar from 5pm, shows
8.30pm Ⓢ 80-90Kč

Palác Akropolis

(4, E9) Labyrinthine entertainment palace with a wealth of alternative, often experimental talent (local and international) on show in its various performance spaces, from Macedonian gypsy bands to hip hop. Has a good cafe and restaurant for when you need to feed your stomach as well as your senses.
✉ Kubelíkova 27, Žižkov ☎ 96 33 09 11
📧 www.palacakropolis
.cz Ⓜ Jiřího Z Poděbrad
🕐 cafe Mon-Fri 10am-midnight, Sat-Sun 4pm-midnight; restaurant 11.30am-1am; bar from 7pm Ⓢ 90-350Kč

Red Hot & Blues

(7, B9) More Tex-Mex dinner show than blues bar or jazz joint, but still pleases the out-of-towners with a mixture of restrained chords, platefuls of Creole cooking and homemade chilli, and bustling service. The courtyard is a great place to raise a glass to a Lazy Pigs Band number.
✉ Jakubská 12, Staré Město ☎ 22 31 46 39
Ⓜ Náměstí Republiky
🕐 9am-midnight, shows 7-10pm Ⓢ free

Rock Café

(3, H6) The rock'n'roll circus has come to town. Over-commercialised to the hilt and loving it, the Rock Café has a cinema showing cult flicks, more merchandising than Michael Jordan, and a vault-like auditorium regularly thrashed to within an inch of its acoustics.

Attracts anachronistic goths and MIB (Men In Black).
✉ Národní 20, Nové Město ☎ 24 91 44 16
📧 www.rockcafe.cz
Ⓜ Národní třída
🕐 Mon-Fri 10am-3am, Sat-Sun 7pm-3am, shows 8.30pm
Ⓢ 50-100Kč

Vagon

(3, H6) Temptingly grungy underground pub with a young Czech crowd, surly bar staff and wall-sketches of Hendrix, Joplin and Zappa etc. There's also a mini-bowling alley. Catch original Czech outfits or revivalist bands, or head to the jam session Tuesday nights.
✉ Národní 25, Nové Město ☎ 21 08 55 99
📧 www.vagon.cz
Ⓜ Národní třída
🕐 Mon-Sat 6pm-5am, Sun 6pm-1am, shows 8.30pm Ⓢ 80Kč

THEATRE

Archa Theatre

(3, C12) Highly regarded staging house for innovative works, predominantly international troupes but Czech artists too. Offerings have included puppetry, tap dancing and contemporary folk music.
✉ Na poříčí 26, Nové Město ☎ 21 71 63 33
📧 www.archatheatre
.cz Ⓜ Náměstí Republiky 🕐 performances 8pm; box office Mon-Fri 10am-6pm, Sat-Sun 2hrs before show Ⓢ 100-500Kč, concessions some shows

Celetná Theatre

(7, C8) In an arcade running between Celetná and Štupartská, the Divadlo v

Celetné is the dramatic abode of the industrious Jiří Srnec Black Light Theatre of Prague. Recent work has included a tribute to the great Pierrot, Jean Gaspard Deburau, and an interpretation of *Flowers for Algernon*. Book ahead.
✉ Celetná 17, Staré Město ☎ 232 68 43
📧 www.divadlo.cz/
celetna Ⓜ Náměstí Republiky 🕐 usually at least one show daily at 7.30pm; box office Mon-Fri 9am-7.30pm, Sat-Sun noon-7.30pm Ⓢ up to 225Kč , concessions some shows ♿

Image Theatre

(7, B5) Creative black-light theatre, with pantomime,

contemporary dance and video – not to mention liberal doses of slapstick – to tell their stories. The staging can be very effective, but the atmosphere is often dictated by audience reaction.
✉ Pařížská 4, Staré Město ☎ 232 91 91
📧 www.imagetheatre.cz
Ⓜ Staroměstská
🕐 performances Mar-Sept 8pm; Oct-Feb Mon-Sat 8pm; box office 9am-8pm Ⓢ 400Kč

Laterna Magika

(3, J4) Since its first cutting-edge show amalgamated stage performance with music, dance and film at the 1958 Brussels World Fair, Laterna Magika has done

Glowing Acts

Contrary to what you might think, 'black-light theatre' does not involve sitting in a hall with the lights turned off, or an experimental play by astrophysicists featuring collapsed stars. Rather, it's a mixture of mime, dance, drama and puppetry performed in front of a black backdrop by ultraviolet-illuminated actors and objects all dressed in phosphorescent garb.

A growing number of places are presenting this theatrical genre in Prague. The more interesting and entertaining companies include the **Jiří Srnec Black Light Theatre of Prague** (see p. 93), **Image Theatre** (see p. 93) and **All Colours Theatre** (Rytířská 31, Staré Město; 7, E7; ☎ 21 61 01 73).

very nicely and now commands the New National Theatre building. It's expensive fare, and popularity has dulled some of the original creative gleam, but mainstream audiences aren't complaining.

✉ **Národní 4, Nové Město** ☎ 24 91 41 29 @ **info@laterna.cz; www.laterna.cz** Ⓜ **Národní třída** ☺ performances Mon-Fri 8pm, Sat 5pm & 8pm; box office Mon-Sat 10am-8pm ⑤ advance bookings 690Kč, walk-ins 600Kč

National Marionette Theatre (7, C3)

Join the throng to watch what is loudly touted as the longest-running classical marionette show in the city, *Don Giovanni*. This operatic, life-sized marionette extravaganza is performed in a 1928 Art Deco theatre and has spawned several imitators around town. Some feel the skilful puppetry gets less impressive after the first 30mins.

✉ **Žatecká 1, Staré Město** ☎ 24 81 93 23 @ **festival@mozart.cz; www.mozart.cz** Ⓜ **Staroměstská** ☺ performances Nov-Feb: Mon & Thurs 8pm; Mar-May & Oct: Mon-Tues & Thurs-Fri 8pm; June-Sept: Thurs-Tues 8pm; box office 10am-8pm ⑤ 490/390Kč ♿

Spiral Theatre (4, B8)

In the sprawling Fairgrounds in Holešovice, this tall black-cloaked space is devoted to Czech-language musicals and theatre, including interpretations of popular non-Czech works like *Romeo & Juliet* (unless there's something Shakespeare wasn't telling us).

✉ **Fairgrounds (Výstaviště), Holešovice** ☎ 20 10 36 24 Ⓜ **Nádraží Holešovice**, then tram 5, 12, 17, 53, 54 to Výstaviště ☺ box office Tues-Sun 3-7pm ⑤ 195-495Kč

Theatre on the Balustrade (7, F1)

Immerse yourself in Czech-language drama at the theatre where Václav Havel honed his skills as a playwright four decades ago. This 'off-Národní' theatre (Divadlo Na zábradlí) dabbled in absurdism early on and now hosts a variety of contemporary material. Deservedly well patronised, usually with a fair crowd ensconced in its cafe.

✉ **Anenské náměstí 5, Staré Město** ☎ 22 22 20 26 @ **marketing@ nazabradli.cz; www.naz abradli.cz** Ⓜ **Staroměstská** ☺ box office 2-7pm ⑤ 90-180Kč, concession of 50% ♿

Theatre Pyramida (4, B8)

Also known as GoJa Music Hall, this is a mainstream pyramid-shaped theatre that puts predictable appeal before creative endeavour by staging failure-proof shows such as *Grease* (in Czech).

✉ **Fairgrounds (Výstaviště), Holešovice** ☎ 22 89 73 33 @ **www.goja.cz** Ⓜ **Nádraží Holešovice**, then tram 5, 12, 17, 53, 54 to Výstaviště ⑤ 120-480Kč ♿

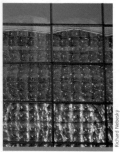

Richard Nebeský

Laterna Magika distorts the imagination.

CLASSICAL MUSIC, OPERA & BALLET

Estates Theatre

(7, D7) This imposing neo-classical building (Stavovské Divadlo) is the oldest theatre in Prague, and its beautifully restored auditorium is still heavily relied on by the National Theatre collective to provide a grand setting for Czech classical music concerts, ballets and operas. Equipped with wheelchair access and good facilities for the hearing-impaired.
✉ Ovocný trh 1, Staré Město ☎ information 24 21 50 01, reservations 24 90 16 38
e www.narodni-divad lo.cz Ⓜ Můstek
⏱ box office (in Kolowrat Palace, Ovocný trh 6) Mon-Fri 10am-6pm, Sat-Sun 10am-12.30pm & 3-6pm; evening box office in theatre open 30mins before performances Ⓢ 200-1000Kč

Liechtenstein Palace

(2, E4) The large seat of Prague's Academy of Music is a pretty good place to catch relatively undemanding collections of musical snippets from popular ballets, operas and symphonies, such as *Famous Romantic Melodies* and *Famous Encores*.
✉ Malostranské náměstí 13, Malá Strana ☎ 33 37 17 15, 0603 52 65 75
Ⓜ Malostranská
⏱ tickets sold at front door 1hr before concerts Ⓢ up to 400Kč

Municipal House

(7, C10) Smetana Hall, centrepiece of the stunning Municipal House (Obecní Dům), is the city's biggest concert hall with a capacity of 1500. It is where the Prague Symphony Orchestra goes to play among statues of famous composers and Karel Špillar paintwork.
✉ náměstí Republiky 5, Staré Město
☎ 22 00 23 36
e www.fok.cz
Ⓜ Náměstí Republiky
⏱ box office (U Obecního domu 2) Mon-Fri 10am-6pm & 1hr before concerts Ⓢ 150-900Kč

National Theatre

(3, J4) Glorious, golden-roofed centrepiece of Czech performing arts institutions, Národní Divadlo is credited with providing a forum for the emancipation of Czech culture. Operatic works by Bedřich Smetana and Antonin Dvořák share the stage with balletic presentations from choreographer Jiří Kylián, plus old favourites like *The Nutcracker*.
✉ Národní 2, Nové Město ☎ information 24 90 14 48, reservations 24 90 16 38
e www.narodni-divad lo.cz Ⓜ Národní třída
⏱ box office Mon-Fri 10am-6pm, Sat-Sun 10am-12.30pm & 3pm-6pm; evening box office in theatre open 30mins before performances Ⓢ 200-1000Kč

Prague State Opera

(3, J12) If you're going to hang out on a balcony, make it one of the neo-rococo perches in the high-culture home of the Prague State Opera (Státní Opera Praha), where you can indulge yourself in melodramatic tones or the occasional ballet. Productions include standards like *Carmen, La Traviata* and *Cosi fan tutte*.
✉ Wilsonova 4, Nové Město ☎ information 0800 135 784, box office 24 22 72 66
e order@ticketsbti.cz; www.opera.cz
Ⓜ Muzeum
⏱ box office Mon-Fri 10am-5.30pm, Sat-Sun 10am-noon & 1-5.30pm Ⓢ 200-950Kč, standing room 100/57Kč for opera/ballet

Richard Nebeský

It ain't opera 'til the fat lady sings.

Just the Ticket

Even up to 30 minutes before a performance starts, you can often still get a ticket at the box office. When booking ahead is advised or you have your rear end primed for a particular seat, the following computerised ticket agencies can help you out – note that you're probably looking at a 10-15% mark-up and some agencies don't take credit cards.

BTI (Bohemia Ticket International) (Malé náměstí 13, Staré Město; 7, D4; ☎ 24 22 78 32, 24 23 77 27; fax 24 21 81 67; e www.ticketsbti.cz)

Ticketpro (Salvátorská 10, Josefov; closed Sat-Sun; 7, A5) or (Old Town Hall, Staré Město; open every day; ☎ 24 81 80 80, 140 51; e www.ticketpro.cz)

FOK (mainly Prague Symphony Orchestra tickets; U Obecního domu 2, Nové Město; 7, B10; ☎ 22 00 23 36; fax 232 25 01; e www.fok.cz)

Rudolfinum (3, C4)
Within the massive neo-Renaissance Rudolfinum you'll find the colonnade-lined Dvořák Hall. This magnificent concert hall is the performance base for the Czech Philharmonic Orchestra and should definitely be one of the 'must-see' places you put on the top of your list. Simply sit back and be impressed by some of the best classical musicians in Prague.
⊠ **náměstí Jana Palacha 1, Josefov**
☎ 24 89 33 52
Ⓜ **Staroměstská**
🕐 box office (Alšovo nábřeží 12) Mon-Fri 10am-6pm & 1hr before concerts
Ⓢ 150-900Kč, concession available most shows

Villa Amerika (4, F8)
Villa Amerika was built in 1717 as a count's immodest summer retreat. These days it's the home of the Dvořák Museum and its salon is used by the Original Music Theatre of Prague as a historical setting for their period-costumed vocal and instrumental show, *Wonderful Dvořák*.
⊠ **Ke Karlovu 20, Nové Město**
☎ 29 82 14
Ⓜ **IP Pavlova**
🕐 Apr-Oct Tues & Fri 8pm Ⓢ 495Kč

CINEMAS

Jalta (3, H10)
Jalta usually has a couple of English-language flicks subtitled in Czech on offer, convenient for when you need some respite from the commercial scramble out on Wenceslas Square.
⊠ **Václavské náměstí 43, Nové Město**
☎ 24 22 88 14
e www.djg.cz/jalta.htm
Ⓜ **Muzeum**
🕐 box office open from 3pm Ⓢ 70-95Kč

Kino 64 U Hradeb
(2, E5) On the edge of a decorous courtyard with a dry fountain behind Maccas, this cinema is predisposed to showing the more mainstream foreign-language films, accompanied by on-screen Czech translations.
⊠ **Mostecká 21, Malá Strana** ☎ 57 53 11 58
Ⓜ **Malostranská**
🕐 box office 2-9.30pm
Ⓢ 110-180Kč

Kino Aero (4, D11)
In a large courtyard surrounded by old apartment buildings, this excellent art-house and classics cinema screens everything from *Monty Python & the Holy Grail* to the highly successful imp-flick *Le fabuleux destin d'Amélie Poulain*. All films in original languages with subtitles.
⊠ **Biskupcova 31, Žižkov** ☎ 71 77 13 49
e www.kinoaero.cz
Ⓜ **Florenc**, then bus 133 to Biskupcova
🕐 box office 5-9pm, bar 4-11pm Ⓢ 60-90Kč, film club screenings require 30Kč membership pass ♿

Kino Perštýn (3, G6)
Downstairs cinema that forgoes those boring old rows of seats for a sociable scattering of tables and chairs. You can smoke in the next-door bar, but only drinks (and not fumes) can accompany you into the cinema. English/foreign-language films with Czech subtitles.
⊠ **Na Perštýně 6, Staré Město** ☎ 21 66 84 32 Ⓜ **Národní třída**

The MAT Studio bar: high gloss inside, flat matt outside.

🕐 box office from 4pm 💲 80-130Kč

Kotva – Broadway

(7, A10) Compact seven-row theatre on the ground floor of Kotva, screening mainly English-language films with Czech subtitles. The ticket price is lowered by 20% for screenings of films that have survived their first release, which means you'll never see *Waterworld* here.

✉ náměstí Republiky 8, Staré Město ☎ 24 82 83 16 Ⓜ Náměstí Republiky 🕐 box office 10.30-11.30am & 1.30-11.30pm 💲 80-100Kč

Lucerna

(3, H9) There's a limited selection of motion pictures at this one-theatre venue, but it exudes a hidden-in-a-passageway charm, and you have to admit there's a certain novelty in asking your friends to meet you under the upside-down horse (see p. 43).

✉ Lucerna Passage, Vodičkova 36, Nové Město ☎ 24 21 69 72 Ⓜ Muzeum 🕐 box office 10am-noon, 1-7.15pm, 7.45-9pm 💲 110Kč

MAT Studio

(4, F7) Former TV studio and private screening venue turned cool cinema, where film types sip espressos and wine in the celluloid-decorated downstairs bar/club or the arty upstairs bistro. Gets bonus hip points for being in a building that looks like a dirty bathroom turned inside out.

✉ Karlovo náměstí 19, Nové Město ☎ 24 91 57 65 🅴 www.mat.cz Ⓜ Karlovo Náměstí 🕐 Mon-Fri 11am-midnight, Sat-Sun 2pm-midnight 💲 60-100Kč ⚢ 30Kč matinee Sat-Sun 3pm

Multikino Cerný Most

(4, B14) Eight-screen Village Cinemas complex out at Černý Most, at the eastern end of the B metro line. No prizes for guessing that it's the Hollywood blockbuster style of movie that kicks cinematic butt here.

✉ Chlumecká 8, Černý Most ☎ 66 79 09 99 🅴 www.villagecine mas.cz Ⓜ Černý Most 🕐 session times roughly noon-10.30pm 💲 139-149/119-129Kč, Mon-Fri before 5pm 109-149/89Kč

Ster Century Multiplex

(7, D10) Ten screens of big-budget, Western-style entertainment in one brightly lit complex. Fortunately there's a wine bar next door where you can drown your sorrow over having paid to see *Pearl Harbour*.

✉ Na příkopě 22, Nové Město ☎ 21 45 12 14 🅴 www.stercentury.cz Ⓜ Náměstí Republiky 🕐 box office Mon-Thurs 11.30am-11pm, Fri 11.30am-12.30am, Sat 9.30am-12.30am, Sun 9.30-11pm 💲 159Kč, family 444Kč ⚢

Moving Pictures

Czech filmmaking blossomed from 1963-68, when graduates of a Communist-run film academy side-stepped censorship. Among them was Miloš Forman, who produced 1963's *Černý Petr* (Black Peter). Jan Svěrák directed two pivotal films: *Kolja* (1996), about a Russian boy reared by a Czech man; and *Tmavomodrý svět* (The Dark-Blue World; 2001), concerning Czech pilots in WWII. David Ondříček released the acclaimed *Samotáři* in 2000, a year that also saw Jan Hrebejk's Academy Award-nominated *Musíme si pomáhat* (Divided We Fall).

International flicks that have been substantially shot in the Czech capital include Forman's *Amadeus*, Barbara Streisand's lukewarmly received *Yentl* and Brian de Palma's *Mission Impossible*.

GAY & LESBIAN PRAGUE

A-Club (4, E10)
This highly rated late-night lesbian bar is tucked away in the back-blocks of Žižkov. Friday night is for women only, while both Friday and Saturday nights are regularly enlivened by a disco.
✉ **Miličova 25, Žižkov**
☎ **22 78 16 23**
Ⓜ **Jiřího Z Poděbrad**
🕐 **7pm-6am** ⓢ **free**

Babylonia (3, H6)
Gay-only sauna which extends itself beyond steam and hot rocks to provide a jacuzzi, fitness room, and massages. To help you achieve a balance between your health-oriented goals and your less-salubrious impulses, there's also a bar.
✉ **Martinská 6, Staré Město** ☎ **24 23 23 04**
ⓔ **www.amigo.cz/ babylonia** Ⓜ **Národní třída** 🕐 **2pm-3am**
ⓢ **gym 60Kč, sauna or gym & sauna 250Kč**

Escape (3, J8)
One of the newest and flashiest gay clubs on the Prague block, amalgamating a late-night restaurant with go-go dancers and a vividly dressed disco. It claims an 'escape to paradise', but for most committed clubbers it will be a reunion. Not to be confused with the cocktail

bar of the same name in the Old Town.
✉ **V Jámě 8, Nové Město** ☎ **0606 538 111**
ⓔ **www.volny.cz/ escapeclub**
Ⓜ **Národní třída**
🕐 **restaurant 7pm-3am, club 10pm-5am**

Fajn Bar (4, F7)
The 'Fine' bar/cafe and its cool pink interior is indeed a decent place to have a leisurely quaff or laid-back chat, though the staff occasionally subvert the relaxed atmosphere with anthemic doof-doof masquerading as music.
✉ **Dittrichova 5, Nové Město** ☎ **24 91 74 09**
Ⓜ **Karlovo Náměstí**
🕐 **Mon-Fri 1pm-1am, Sun 2pm-1am**

Friends (3, G4)
Good cellar spot to sit back and sip some wine or coffee, or to join in the busy spirit of assorted theme nights. These can include Czech music, movies or one for the oldies; DJs add their own spin Wednesday to Saturday.
✉ **Náprstkova 1, Staré Město** ☎ **21 63 54 08**
ⓔ **www.friends-prague .cz** Ⓜ **Národní třída**
🕐 **4pm-3am**

Gejzeer (6, B4)
Large gay and lesbian club

that draws an equally large crowd to its dual bars and disco. Besides the usual dance and video-related activities, Gejzeer seems keen to play matchmaker by offering 'meet a partner' nights and its equally euphemistic 'darkroom'.
✉ **Vinohradská 40, Vinohrady** ☎ **22 51 60 36** ⓔ **www.volny.cz/ gejzeer** Ⓜ **Náměstí Miru** 🕐 **Tues-Thurs 6pm-4am, Fri-Sat 9pm-5am, club music 11.30pm** ⓢ **Tues-Thurs free, Fri free to 10.30pm then 100Kč, Sat free to 10.30pm then 150Kč**

Pinocchio (4, E9)
Sizeable confluence of gay clubbers with a lively gambling room, strip show-enhanced bar, and a very popular disco that leaves you with a neon afterglow. Upstairs is a gay hotel (separate entry) with a dozen basic but well-maintained rooms.
✉ **Seifertova 3, Žižkov**
☎ **22 71 07 76, 0602 969 374**
ⓔ **www.volny.cz/ pinocchio**
Ⓜ **Hlavní Nádraží**
🕐 **3pm-6am** ⓢ **free**

Pivnice U Rudolfa
(3, K10) Gay beer hall with cosy subground surrounds, all of it a convenient waddle from Muzeum metro. You'll find that this place is at its best when you feel like animated company rather than thoughtful solitude.
✉ **Mezibranská 3, Nové Město** ☎ **0605 872 492** Ⓜ **Muzeum**
🕐 **4pm-2am**

Prague boasts a high-spirited gay and lesbian scene.

Richard Nebesky

SPECTATOR SPORT

Prague International Marathon

The annual 42km Prague International Marathon first hit the streets in 1989 and now attracts more foreigners than locals. The full run – from Old Town Square around Josefov, over Charles Bridge, south down Malá Strana and then back up to the square – is usually staged in the latter half of May, and a half-marathon is held mid-March. If you fancy your chances, the times to beat are 2:26:33 for women and 2:08:52 for men.

Ice Hockey

Czechs love ice hockey *(lední hokey)*. They've won 10 world titles, most recently in 2001. There are 14 teams in the national league, including the successful Sparta Praha and Slavia Praha, but for several years the competition has been a one-puck race led by a team from Vsetin. A good place to catch the action is **Paegas Arena**, Sparta Praha's home rink.

Football

In August-December and February-June, AC Sparta Praha competes with itself to see how many points clear at the top of the ladder it will be by the domestic season's end. Although this team is occasionally pressed by rivals, it usually makes a lot of vocal football *(fotbal)* followers ecstatic by the competition's conclusion. Catch a game at the **AC Sparta Praha stadium**.

Tennis

The main venue in town for high-profile tennis *(tenis)* events is the **Štvanice club**, which usually stages the annual Czech Open and has also hung out the nets for Davis Cup matches. But the glory days of the inexhaustible Martina Navrátilová and the man with the Easter Island scowl, Ivan Lendl, are long gone – as are their respective Czech citizenships.

Horse Racing

If racing *(dostihy)* is your scene, head down to the horse-pounded turf at **Chuchle závodiště**. Races are generally run between May and October, on Tuesday and Sunday from 2pm onwards. The inexpensive tickets should be available at the racecourse *(závodiště)*.

Offices & Venues

- **Prague International Marathon** (5th fl, Záhořanského 3, Nové Město; 4, F7; ☎ 24 91 92 09; e www.pim.cz; Ⓜ Karlovo náměstí)
- **HC Sparta Praha (Paegas Arena)** (Za Elektrárnou 419, Bubeneč; 4, C8; ☎ 872 74 11; e www.hcsparta.cz; Ⓜ Nádraží Holešovice then tram 5, 12, 17, 53 or 54 to Výstaviště)
- **AC Sparta Praha stadium** (Milady Horákové 98, Bubeneč; 4, C7; ☎ 20 57 03 23; e www.sparta.cz; Ⓜ Hradčanská then tram 1, 8, 25, 26, 51 or 56 to Sparta)
- **Štvanice club** (TJ Slavoj Praha; ostrov S38; 4, D9; ☎ 24 81 78 07; 🚊 3, 26, 56 to Vltavská)
- **Chuchle závodiště** (Radotínská 69, Velká Chuchle; 4, K6; ☎ 57 94 10 42; Ⓜ Smíchovské Nádraží then bus 129 or 172 to Chuchle závodiště)

places to stay

Rubberneckers flock to Prague year-round but mainly between April and October, and particularly over Easter, Christmas and New Year, when they eagerly consume large portions of the available accommodation. It's better to book your lodgings as far ahead as possible during these times, and when your trip bumps into local and European public holidays.

The terms 'budget accommodation' and 'city centre' are almost mutually exclusive in Prague, bar a few cheap hostels and hotels within camera-lens distance of Old Town Square. The majority of budget places, where you'll usually find crowded dorms or ultra-plain rooms with shared bathroom, are scattered outside Staré Město – most are in southern Nové Město, east in Vinohrady, and north across the Vltava in Holešovice. Many pensions *(penzións)*, traditionally private boarding houses, can turn out to be hotels attempting a mum-and-dad appeal – some of the genuine ones have homey surrounds, though these tend to be in outer areas.

Mid-range options are often three-star hotels (star ratings are self-applied) with their own restaurant, cafe and/or bar, and rooms equipped with bathroom, satellite TV, phone and minibar; some overcharge foreigners for poorly maintained premises. Meanwhile, there's no shortage of top-end choices stuffed full of classy eateries, grand fittings and business facilities.

A growing trend involves inner-city dwellers doing apartment renovations (sometimes minimalist) and then renting them out to travellers for short or long-term stays. If you go for a flat in the more trampled bits of the Old Town, make sure your bedroom isn't facing the street – late-night revellers tend to treat the narrow streets as their own private karaoke studio. And when inquiring about apartments, take a good hard look at the location, as many are right out in the suburbs. If you want to do your own leg-work, head out to your preferred area and look for signs saying *privát* or *Zimmer frei* (rooms for rent).

Prague's grand old dame, the Hotel Pa

DELUXE

Casa Marcello (3, B8)
Enigmatically hidden behind St Castlus and renovated backwards, so that it's just like it was in the 13th century, except for the satellite TVs, minibars and sauna. Antiques mix it with modern fittings and very comfortable beds in elegant rooms.
✉ **Řásnovka 783, Josefov** ☎ **22 31 02 60; fax 22 31 33 23**
e booking@casa-marcello.cz; www.casa-marcello.cz Ⓜ **Náměstí Republiky** ✕ **Agnes** ♿

Indulge in the Art of Deco at the Radisson Hotel.

Four Seasons Hotel (7, C1) An executive villa for all seasons, freshly opened beside the soporific Vltava and eager to please all-comers with sumptuous yet pragmatic rooms with Internet access, massage on call, a health club and a concierge whose job description includes the word 'resourceful'.
✉ **Veleslavínova 2a, Staré Město** ☎ **21 42 70 00; fax 21 42 60 00**
e www.fourseasons.com Ⓜ **Staroměstská** ✕ **Allegro** ♿

Grand Hotel Bohemia (7, C9)
It may have an antique exterior and a neobaroque ballroom, but this is a thoroughly modern member of an Austrian hotel chain, with efficient service and spacious, if business-like, rooms. Kids 7-12 years of age are charged 50% less; children under six stay free of charge.
✉ **Královdorská 4, Staré Město** ☎ **24 80 41 11; fax 232 95 45**
e www.austria-hotels.co.at/grandhotel-bohemia Ⓜ **Náměstí Republiky** ✕

Hotel Paříž (7, B10)
Bastion of Art Nouveau grandeur circa 1904, now with essential 21st-century mod-cons like heated bathroom floors and massage facilities. Rooms have the requisite bygone era trimmings but remain plushly modern. If you're not staying here, poke your head into the elegant stairwell to see its hand-painted motifs.
✉ **U Obecního domu 1, Staré Město** ☎ **22 19 51 95; fax 24 22 54 75**
e booking@hotel-pariz.cz; www.hotel-pariz.cz Ⓜ **Malostranská, then tram 22 or 23 to Pohořelec** ✕ **Restaurant Sarah Bernhardt (p. 81); Café de Paris** ♿

Hotel Savoy (5, C2)
Has creatively elegant rooms, plus a leather-bound library and a skylit restaurant. It caters to the image-stressed traveller by providing fitness trainers, hairdressers and a gym. Surprisingly, only one room is barrier-free. Pets are accommodated for around 430Kč per animal.
✉ **Keplerova 6, Hradčany** ☎ **24 30 24 30; fax 24 30 21 28**
e info@hotel-savoy.cz; www.hotel-savoy.cz Ⓜ **Malostranská** ✕ **Hradčany Restaurant** ♿

Radisson SAS Alcron Hotel (3, J9)
Five-star Art Deco chic favoured by diplomats and the in-crowd, continuing the legacy that began with the building's first incarnation as the jazzy Alcron Hotel in 1930. Period furnishings and fittings compete for attention with mod-cons and the snappy can-do attitude of the staff.
✉ **Štěpánská 40, Nové Město** ☎ **22 82 00 00; fax 22 82 01 20**
e sales@radissonsas.com; www.radissonsas.com Ⓜ **Muzeum** ✕ **Alcron (p. 74); La Rotonde** ♿

Renaissance Prague Hotel (3, D11)

This upmarket hotel caters particularly well to the business traveller by offering professional service, work-ready rooms, and a business centre with photocopying, printing and a typing service. Also has a fitness centre with a 5m 'endless' pool.
✉ V celnici 7, Nové Město ☎ 21 82 21 00; fax 21 82 22 00 e renaissance.prague@renaissance.cz; www.renaissancehotels.com Ⓜ Náměstí Republiky ✗ Pavillion; U Korbele ⚥

Rezidence Lundborg (3, E1)

Accommodating a collision of the old and new, this refurbished 700-year-old house looks towards historic Charles Bridge and has gleaming contemporary suites, each with its own kitchen and free Internet access. Great family or group base.
✉ U lužického semináře 3, Malá Strana ☎ 57 01 19 11; fax 57 01 19 66 e rezidence@lundborg.cz; www.lundborg.se Ⓜ Malostranská ✗ Pasha (p. 73) ⚥

U Zlaté studně (2, C5)

Commandeering one end of a narrow winding lane, this Renaissance edifice crams in a lot of antique-enhanced luxury. City vistas prompt fantasies of the 'one day all this will be yours' variety, particularly from the restaurant's glorious outdoor terrace.
✉ U Zlaté Studně 4, Malá Strana ☎ 57 01 12 13; fax 57 53 33 20 e hotel@zlatastudna.cz; www.zlatastudna.cz Ⓜ Malostranská ✗ Restaurant U Zlaté studně

TOP END

Arcotel Teatrino (4, E10)

Located in the still predominantly working-class but now alternative arts-flavoured neighbourhood of Žižkov, this one-time theatre has well-appointed rooms. Its centrepiece is a grand Art Nouveau hall where diners and barflys now tread the boards instead of actors.
✉ Bořivojova 53, Žižkov ☎ 21 42 21 11; fax 21 42 22 22 e teatrino@arcotel.at; www.arcote.at Ⓜ Jiřího Z Poděbrad ✗ Teatrino

Domus Henrici (5, C4)

This hotel is intentionally nondescript out the front, hinting that peace and privacy are the top priorities here. Stylish rooms – half of which have a desk, Internet point and fax/copier/scanner for work-occupied visitors – spill out onto terraces which have sigh-inducing views out over Prague.
✉ Loretánská 11, Hradčany ☎ 20 51 13 69; fax 20 51 15 02 e hotel@domus-henrici.cz; www.domus-henrici.cz Ⓜ Malostranská, then tram 22 or 23 to Pohořec ✗ U císařů (p. 70) ⚥

Hotel Astoria (7, A9)

Pleasant apartment-block hotel, architecturally unobtrusive (though being next to Kotva makes that easy). It's one of the newer top-end hotels in the city centre, and its welcoming staff haven't had time to become jaded professionals. Ask for a room on the 7th floor, which will come with a balcony for no extra cost.
✉ Rybná 10, Staré Město ☎ 21 77 57 11; fax 21 77 57 12 e info@hotelastoria.cz; www.hotelastoria.cz Ⓜ Náměstí Republiky ✗ Astoria

Accommodation Agencies

Listed are some reputable accommodation agencies, between them covering everything from hostels to luxury hotels. Many agencies prefer you pay first and then see a place, whereas you'll probably want it the other way around – if in doubt, be persistent.

AVE (offices at airport & main train station; ☎ 51 55 10 11; fax 24 22 34 63; e www.avetravel.cz)
ESTEC Travel Agency (Vaníčkova 5, Strahov; 4, E5; ☎ 57 21 04 10; fax 57 21 52 63; e estec@jrc.cz)
Top Tour (Rybná 3, Staré Město; 7, B9; ☎ 24 81 91 11; fax 24 81 14 00)
Universitas Tour (Opletalova 38, Nové Město; 3, E13; ☎ 22 24 25 34; fax 24 21 22 90)

Catering for Kids

Most places can provide child-sized cots or beds, and most of those with on-site restaurants can handle the concept of smaller portions. Facilities for kids to amuse themselves, however, are almost exclusively found in top-end places, and usually come in the form of the odd board game and video distraction. In-house child minding exists only in the realm of the most upmarket.

If it's any consolation, lots of places will put kids under six or seven years of age up for the night for free – check what arrangements may apply when you book.

Hotel Elite (3, J6)

Guests sleep underneath frescos or paint-daubed wooden beams in this classically refurbished house. And when the antique fittings close in on you, try hitting the refreshing atrium bar. Has the full gamut of services, including secretarial, laundry and a beauty parlour, and is only a block from the shops of Národní třída.
✉ **Ostrovní 32, Nové Město ☎ 24 93 22 50; fax 24 93 07 87**
e **sales@hotelelite.cz; www.hotelelite.cz**
Ⓜ **Národní třída**
✕ **Ultramarin**

Hotel Hoffmeister

(3, B2) Named after celebrity-loving caricaturist Adolf Hoffmeister, whose work adorns a gallery here. Like the hotel generally, rooms can be a bit stuffy and overdressed (with a preponderance of pleats and heavy light fittings) but staff are very attentive and the old castle steps conveniently beckon nearby.
✉ **Pod Bruskou 7, Hradčany ☎ 51 01 71 11; fax 51 01 71 00**
e **hotel@hoffmeister .cz; www.hoffmeister.cz**
Ⓜ **Malostranská** ✕ **Ada**

Hotel Kampa (3, G1)

In this Best Western medieval theme park you'll find that subtlety is an unknown quantity, particularly in the feasting hall buried beneath candelabras and suits of armour. However, the rooms are surprisingly modern and you'll find yourself in one of the less-trammelled parts of the Small Quarter.
✉ **Všehrdova 16, Malá Strana ☎ 57 32 05 08; fax 57 32 02 62**
e **hotel.kampa@vol .cz; www.euroagentur .cz** Ⓜ **Národní třída, then tram 22, 23 or 57 to Újezd** ✕ **Knight Hall ☗**

Hotel Liberty (3, G7)

This antique reproduction-riddled newcomer attracts attitude-riddled jetsetters. It has a convenient location, but reception staff strive to make indifference an Olympic sport. Despite the rather unexceptional rooms, the hotel motto is 'where the rooms have not only a number, but also a soul', which we guess means you can check out, but you can never leave.
✉ **28.října 11, Nové Město ☎ 24 23 95 98; fax 24 23 76 94**
e **info@hotelliberty.cz;**
www.hotelliberty.cz
Ⓜ **Můstek** ✕ **Le Patio (p. 76)**

Hotel U Prince (7, D5)

Accommodation-wise, you won't get closer to Old Town Square unless you camp at the feet of Jan Hus. Recently renovated, this ornate hotel lacks the vast spaces common in other top-end places and has only six rooms per floor, giving it a personalised feel. Beware the wallet-savaging restaurant.
✉ **Staroměstské náměstí 29, Staré Město ☎ 24 21 38 07; fax 24 21 38 07** e **reserve@ hotel uprince.cz; www.hotel uprince.cz**
Ⓜ **Staroměstská**
✕ **Toscana (p. 82) ☗**

Maximilian Hotel

(3, C8) This classically furnished, servicing-your-every-need hotel has a peaceful setting in Josefov's narrow-laned backyard, and is well-patronised by businessfolk, and by wealthy European non-hoi polloi. Heavily insulated rooms mean you're the only one who can delight in your young child's voice.
✉ **Haštalská 14, Josefov ☎ 21 80 61 17; fax 21 80 61 10**

[e] maximilianhotel@
hotmail.com [M] Nám-
ěstí Republiky [X] Chez
Marcel (p. 71) [symbol]

Romantik Hotel U raka (5, A2)

Charming terracotta-roofed
hideaway sheltering
beneath the old city walls.
Preserves its secluded
romantic ambience with a
minimalist attitude to
guests (only six rooms) and
a quiet ignorance of kids
(none under 10 years of
age are allowed). Rooms

Romantik by name, romantik by nature...

are often booked out
months in advance.
[envelope] **Černínská 10** [phone] **20
51 11 00; fax 20 51 05
11** [e] **uraka@login.cz;**
**www.romantikhotels
.com** [M] **Malostranská,**
then tram 22 or 23 to
Pohořelec [X] **U zlaté
hrušky (p. 70)**

MID-RANGE

Botel Albatros (3, A10)

This hotel has an unfortu-
nate choice of seafaring
name. Don't think *QE2*,
think weathered barge
with a Bavarian overhaul.
It's perfect for those who
like the idea of waking up
on the water and not pay-
ing through their stern for
the privilege. The Spartan
cabins are often snaffled
by tour groups, so make
sure you book ahead.
[envelope] **nábřeží Ludvíka
Svobody, Nové Město**
[phone] **24 81 05 41; fax 24
81 12 14** [e] **albatros@
mbox.vol.cz** [M] **Náměstí
Republiky** [X] **Govinda
Vegetarian Club (p. 76)**

Hotel Amadeus

(4, G8) Peachy premises
with a couple of small,
split-level apartments for
those who want to pretend
they're staying in a pent-
house. It may not seem
convenient for lightning
shopping trips or bar-
hopping, but the nearby
metro will whisk you into
the centre in no time.
[envelope] **Slavojova 8,
Vyšehrad**

[phone]**/fax 22 51 17 77,
69 27 32 02**
[e] **jana.dyrsmidova@
telecom.cz; www.hotel
.cz/amadeus-hotel**
[M] **Vyšehrad**
[X] **Na Vyšehradě**

Hotel Ariston (4, E9)

This pleasant-enough
mid-range option is on a
constantly bustling thor-
oughfare. If you stay here,
don't just limit your move-
ments to flitting to and
from the centre; take the
opportunity to explore the
absorbing down-to-earth
neighbourhood of Žižkov.
[envelope] **Seifertova 65, Žižkov**
[phone] **22 78 25 17; fax 22
78 03 47** [M] **Jiřího Z
Poděbrad** [X] [symbol]

Hotel Central (7, A9)

Whoever designed Central's
reception had a passion for
'70s discos, and riding the
claustrophobic faux-marble
lift is like being in a Renaissance mineshaft, but the
simple rooms are cosy and
for an extra 300Kč you can
take your pooch upstairs.
[envelope] **Rybná 8, Staré
Město** [phone] **24 81 20 41;**

fax 232 84 04
[e] **central@orfea.cz**
[M] **Náměstí Republiky**
[X] **Pivnice Radegast
(p. 80)**

Hotel Cloister Inn

(3, G5) The inn looks like
a weary council flat from
the outside, but that just
masks the fact that there
are very pleasantly appoint-
ed rooms within. Located a
few minutes' stumble from
Old Town Square, it's on
the site of a medieval convent no less; book early to
guarantee absolution.
[envelope] **Konviktská 14, Staré
Město** [phone] **24 21 10 20;
fax 24 21 08 00**
[e] **cloister@cloister-inn
.cz; www.cloister-inn.cz**
[M] **Národní třída**
[X] **Café Louvre (p. 75)**

Hotel Europa (3, H9)

It still catches your eye
with its striking Art
Nouveau frontage, but the
internal grandeur has sunk
past acceptably tatty into
forlornness. Even so, you
could do a lot worse than
one of the weathered,
balcony-equipped rooms

with a view down into the bustle of Wenceslas Square.

✉ **Václavské náměstí 25, Nové Město** ☎ 24 22 81 17; fax 24 22 45 44 Ⓜ Můstek ✕ Café Europa; 2 restaurants

Hotel Na Zlatém Kříži (3, G8)

The hotel 'On the Golden Cross' – 'golden cross' being estate agent-speak for the seedy intersection of 28.října and Wenceslas Square – has a warm, wood-enhanced feel and is cheap for the city centre. There are only two (slightly musty) rooms on each floor, so make sure you book early; note there's no elevator.

✉ **Jungmannovo náměstí 2, Nové Město** ☎ 24 21 95 01; fax 22 24 54 18 e info@gold encross.cz; www.golden cross.cz Ⓜ Můstek ✕ Káva Káva Káva (p. 76)

Hotel Olea (6, E3)

This old-style hotel favours shades of grey and brown, with some enormous multiroom suites that give you plenty of places to stow the kids and those extra suitcases full of Bohemian crystal. The Hotel Olea has a great, peaceful location for exploring the burgeoning Vinohrady scene.

✉ **Americká 16, Vinohrady** ☎ 22 51 56 91; fax 22 51 56 91 e olea@avetravel.cz; www.avetravel.cz Ⓜ Náměstí Míru ✕ Portobello Road

Hotel Sax (2, E2)

Down a flight of old stairs from Nerudova is this friendly, ultra-contemporary hotel. Despite planting itself firmly in the present, the Hotel Sax is refreshingly low-key, from its tidy, uncluttered rooms and naturally lit atrium to its understated entry marquee.

✉ **Jánský vršek 3, Malá Strana** ☎ 57 53 12 68; fax 57 53 41 01 e hotelsax@giraffe.cz; www.hotelsax.cz Ⓜ Malostranská ✕ U Zeleného Čaje

Penzion U Medvídků (3, H6)

Fans of ceiling artwork (Renaissance of course) and beer halls (there's actually one on the premises) should get on the Web and reserve a spot here as soon as possible. The pension also boasts a sterling location, though you can expect the occasional loud satisfied noise from departing brewery patrons.

✉ **Na Perštýně 7, Staré Město** ☎ 24 21 19 16; fax 24 22 09 30 e info@umedvidku.cz; www.umedvidku.cz Ⓜ Národní třída ✕ Restaurace U Medvídků (p. 80)

U krále Jiřího (7, F2)

'King George's' is a 14th-century edifice with smallish, simple rooms that have been recently refurbished (mead stains mopped up, armour stowed etc). It's within lurching distance of Old Town Square but the bar is so cosy you may not venture outside. Unfortunately there's no lift, only some steep stairs.

✉ **Liliová 10, Staré Město** ☎ 22 22 09 25; fax 22 22 17 07 e kral .jiri@telecom.cz; www .kinggeorge.cz Ⓜ Staroměstská ✕ Reykjavík (p. 81)

U zlaté studny (7, D3)

The 16th-century 'Golden Well' house – no relation to the one in Malá Strana – and its beautifully sculpted frontage yields six large rooms and suites with old-style furniture and exposed beams. They're in demand, so give the helpful front desk a call well in advance.

✉ **Karlova 3, Staré Město** ☎ 22 22 01 30; fax 22 22 01 30 e uzlatestudny@volny .cz; www.uzlatestudny .cz Ⓜ Staroměstská ✕ U zlaté studny

The glitz is gone, but the Europa puts on a flash face.

Richard Nebeský

BUDGET

Hotel/Pension City
(6, E2) Clean, cheap and with a simple aesthetic, hence the panelling in reception that by all rights belongs on the outside of a Winnebago. The main difference between the pension and hotel rooms is a private bathroom in the former; mod cons like TV and phone cost a little extra. Good news for the animal kingdom – pets are welcome.
✉ Belgická 10, Vinohrady ☎ 22 52 16 06; fax 22 52 23 86
e hotel@hotelcity.cz; www.hotelcity.cz
Ⓜ Náměstí Míru ✕ FX Café (p. 83) ♿

Hotel Imperial
(3, C12) The cavernous corridors and rarefied air of the brooding Imperial may be perfect for *The Shining 2*, and its rooms may be furnished with what looks like unsold garage sale stock, but it has a certain dignified

---

Pet-Friendly

Following are a few of the hotels and pensions around Prague that are willing to help save you the heartbreak of putting your trusty nonhuman companion into a facility where they're treated like royalty while you're away: **Hotel Savoy** (p. 101), **Hotel Central** (p. 104), **Hotel/Pension City** (see this page), and **Unitas Pension** (see this page).

---

atmosphere (note the wonderful mosaics in the *kavárna*) and is dirt cheap considering the location.
✉ Na Poříčí 15, Nové Město ☎ 231 60 12; fax 231 60 12
e into@hotelimperial .cz; www.hotelimperial .cz Ⓜ Náměstí Republiky ✕ Café Imperial

Hotel Rococo (4, F7)
We couldn't find where they hid the rococo, but while searching saw cosy rooms and an outdoor area where you can sit and prepare for the shortish walk to Wenceslas Square. This is the upper end of budget, with discounts likely outside peak times.
✉ Salmovská 14, Nové Město ☎ 24 92 27 27; fax 24 92 27 27
e hotel.rococo@quick .cz; www.hotelrococo .cz Ⓜ Karlovo Náměstí ✕ Miyabi (p. 77)

Pension Museum
(3, K10) This is a very nice pension with 24-hour reception, right off the hubbub of Wenceslas Square and with rooms sheltered from urban reality in a peaceful courtyard. The only disappointing aspect is that there's just a handful of rooms, including one that's wheelchair-accessible.
✉ Mezibranská 15, Nové Město ☎ 96 32 51 86; fax 96 32 51 88
e www.pension-muzeum.cz Ⓜ Muzeum ✕ Mayur Indický (p. 77)

Pension Vltava
(4, C9) The worn, landlocked rooms strangely feel like they belong on an old boat. But despite this, it's extremely friendly, aquamarine has been splashed around to brighten it up, and the entrance-way makes you feel like you're attending a cabal – frankly, that makes it worth the low admission price.
✉ Dělnická 35, Holešovice ☎ 80 97 95; fax 80 97 95
Ⓜ Nádraží Holešovice

Sir Toby's Hostel
(4, C9) This exemplary smoke-free hostel (puffers have to head for the balconies) has the brightest facade on the street. It's been recently spruced up inside and out and is planning further development of facilities. Very accommodating staff can provide info on the neighbourhood and Prague in general.
✉ Dělnická 24, Holešovice ☎ 83 87 06 35; fax 80 82 89
e www.sirtobys.com
Ⓜ Nádraží Holešovice

Unitas Pension
(3, H5) Every man, woman and their dog are welcome here. Apparently, you can eschew a private room for a bunk in a former secret police prison cell – personally we fail to see the attraction. Managed by Cloister Inn, the pension was due for renovation at the time of writing, so prices may have risen.
✉ Bartolomějská 9, Staré Město ☎ 24 21 10 20; fax 24 21 08 00
e unitas@cloister-inn .cz; www.pensionunitas .com Ⓜ Národní třída ✕ Konvikt Pub

facts for the visitor

Richard Nebesky

A fine vintage: catch an old red rattler to see the sights.

ARRIVAL & DEPARTURE

Around 30 international carriers jet in to Prague's international airport, Ruzyně. There are direct flights from most major European cities, including London, Paris, Amsterdam and Frankfurt. Nearly all extra-Continental flights, however, are routed through another European city. Domestically, you can fly from Prague to Brno and Ostrava.

Bus services converge on the Czech capital from destinations throughout Europe. Ditto trains, which arrive from rail hubs like Amsterdam, Munich and Paris.

Air

Praha Ruzyně airport (4, D1) is about 15km west of the city centre, accessible by a combination of bus and metro. The main building shelters an arrival hall and a departure hall. Facilities include a bar, fast-food places, basic Internet access, several travel and accommodation agencies, and a scattering of ATMs and money exchange offices.

Left Luggage

There is a 24hr left-luggage service in the Arrivals Hall that charges 40Kč per piece of luggage.

Information

General Inquiries	☎ 2011 1111
	☎ 2011 3314
Flight Information	
ČSA	☎ 2011 1111
Air France	☎ 2011 3737
British Airways	☎ 2011 4421
KLM	☎ 2011 4148
Lufthansa	☎ 2011 4456
Car Park Information	☎ 2011 3408

Hotel Booking Service
Čedok (☎ 2011 3744; e cedok-airport@cedok.cz); AVE (☎ 20 56 18 17; e www.avetravel.cz)

Airport Access

Public transport information is available from Ruzyně airport office in the city transport department (Dopravní podnik, or DP; ☎ 20 11 54 04; e www.dp-praha.cz).

Bus & Metro From in front of the airport's main building, catch bus No 119 or No 254 to Dejvická metro station, then ride line A into the centre; the trip takes about 45 minutes. Alternatively, bus Nos 179 and 225 run to Nové Butovice metro station in Prague's south-west, from where line B heads into town.

Bus & Tram Between midnight and 3.30am, catch night bus No 510 and transfer to city-bound tram No 51 at Divoká Šárká stop.

Taxi There's a desk in the Arrivals Hall for Airport Cars (☎ 2011 38 92; open 8am-11pm); no other taxis can stop outside the Arrivals Hall. A trip into the city will cost upwards of a pricey 600Kč per person, depending on the destination. From Old Town Square in a regular taxi, you'll pay around 450-500Kč to the airport.

Minibus Vans operated by Cedaz (☎ 20 11 42 96) run between the airport and náměstí Republiky for 90Kč per person. The vehicles can also be commissioned to drive from the airport to anywhere in the centre for 360Kč for up to four people (720Kč five-eight people). Cedaz operates from the airport from 6am-9pm, and from náměstí Republiky 5.30am-9.30pm.

Bus

The state bus company, Czech Automobile Transport (ČSAD), operates regional and long-distance domestic coaches from Florenc bus station (3, D14). Information is available 6am-9pm in Florenc's central hall at window No 8, or online (e www.jizdnirady.cz).

Numerous international coaches service Prague, including a Czech line handled by Bohemia Euroexpress International (Koněvova 126; 4, D11; ☎ 22 71 85 49; e www.bei.cz), and those belonging to the Eurolines consortium, whose main Prague agent is Sodeli CZ (Senovážné náměstí 6; 3, F11; ☎ 24 23 93 18). The majority of coaches operate from stands at Florenc bus station and Želivského metro station (4, F11), and also from one at Nádraží Holešovice metro station.

Call ☎ 129 99 for information on bus connections.

Train

Inexpensive and reliable domestic services are provided by Czech Railways (ČD). You can buy plain tickets (jízdenka) or tickets with a reservation (místenka) for a seat, couchette or sleeper; when scanning timetables, look out for services designated 'R' (reservations recommended) or a circled/boxed 'R' (reservations mandatory).

Most international trains pull up at the multilevel mayhem that is Prague's main train station, Praha Hlavní Nádraží (3, G13; ☎ 24 61 52 49), though some end up at stations at Smíchov (4, G6) and Holešovice (4, B9). For information on rail connections, call ☎ 24 22 42 00 or visit the website e www.cdrail.cz.

Travel Documents

Passport

Those requiring a visa to visit the Czech Republic must have a passport valid for at least three months longer than the validity of the visa.

Visa

Nationals of the United Kingdom can stay in the Czech Republic for 180 days without a visa, while nationals of other EU countries plus New Zealand and Ireland can visit visa-free for 90 days. US citizens can visit without a visa for 30 days. Australians, Canadians and South Africans have to apply to a Czech embassy or consulate for a tourist visa (visas are no longer issued at the airport or border crossings): 90-day single/multiple entry visas cost US$22/82 for Americans and US$49/98 for Canadians, while Australians are charged a fixed rate of US$38.

Return/Onward Ticket

A return or onward ticket is usually (but for some reason not always) required to gain entry to the Czech Republic.

Customs

Visitors can import or export unlimited amounts of foreign currency, but only up to 200,000Kč in Czech currency.

Duty Free

You can import 2L of wine, 1L of spirits and 200 cigarettes without paying duty, as well as gifts (noncommercial goods) collectively worth under 6000Kč; quantities of these goods over the specified limits have to be declared on arrival. Treat that potential antique buy of a lifetime with caution, as the real deal cannot be exported. And when on a shopping spree, remember that purchases exceeding 30,000Kč attract a 22% duty.

Departure Tax

Departure taxes are included in the price of your air ticket.

GETTING AROUND

Prague's cheap, extensive and relatively easy public transport system is run by its transport department (Dopravní podnik; e www.dp-praha.cz), which maintains information centres at the airport and in five metro stations, including Muzeum (3, J10; ☎ 22 62 37 77; open 7am-9pm) and Můstek (3, G8; ☎ 22 64 63 50; open 7am-9pm). Most visitors rely on the underground metro to sweep them from one side of the city to the other. Trams are also convenient, with 26 daytime routes and a handful of night-time services negotiating all the main inner city areas. Buses are mostly useful for filling in the urban gaps in the metro and tram systems, as they cover pretty much everywhere beyond the centre. Pick up the detailed *Guide to Prague Public Transport* pamphlet from an information office.

Single transfer tickets (12/6Kč) are good for all public transport for 60mins from the moment you punch them into a validation machine (for 90mins Mon-Fri 8pm-5am and Sat-Sun all day). Single non-transfer tickets (8/4Kč) are for short hops lasting no more than 15mins on buses and trams, or up to four metro stations; they are not valid for the funicular or for night transport. Tickets can be bought from ticket machines in the metro stations and at newsstands, various hotels and travel agencies.

Travel Passes

Most short-stay visitors will find it cost-effective to buy tickets as they need them. If you anticipate jumping on/off public transport more than half-a-dozen times a day over an extended period, you should buy a short-term season pass allowing unlimited use of the metro, trams, buses and the Petřín funicular for 1/3/7/15 days at a cost of 70/200/250/280Kč. Long-term season passes give you 1/3/12 months of transport time for 420/1150/3800Kč, with a 50% student discount available for the monthly and quarterly tickets. Don't forget to validate these passes the first time you use them.

Metro

The swift, 49-station metro operates 5am-midnight and comprises three lines, each identified by both a letter and a colour: A (green), B (yellow) and C (red). To leave a station, head for a sign saying *výstup* (exit); for a connecting line, look for a *přestup*. Disabled travellers should note that barrierless access to platforms is more a feature of suburban metro stations than inner city ones, the exceptions being Muzeum and Hlavní Nádraží.

Tram & Bus

The numbers allocated to tram lines have 1-2 digits, while bus route numbers have three digits. During the 'day', trams and buses run 4.30am-12.15am, with more limited but still fairly regular 'night' services in the intervening time; night-time routes are serviced by buses numbered 501-512. The info centres in Muzeum, Můstek, Anděl, Černý Most and Nádraží Holešovice metro stations supply timetables and route maps for the tram and bus systems.

Funicular

The funicular railway tackles the steep climb from Újezd to the top of Petřín Hill and is part of Prague's integrated transport system. The cost of a one-way trip is 12/6Kč and the service runs every 10-15mins 9.15am-8.45pm.

Taxi

Unfortunately Prague has an over-supply of crooked taxi drivers who do a major disservice to the honest ones. Unless you want to be grossly overcharged, don't flag down a cab or use a taxi-stand in any of the main tourist areas. Instead, call one of these usually reliable 24hr radio-taxis: AAA Radio Taxi (☎ 140 14, 33 11 33 11); Cedaz (☎ 20 11 42 96); City Taxi (33 10 33 10); or ProfiTaxi (☎ 61 31 41 51).

If you try your luck on the street, confirm the fare and check that the meter is working before getting in. Flagfall should be a maximum 30Kč and 22Kč per kilometre after that.

Car & Motorcycle

Driving calmly through the narrow, cobblestoned streets of the historic district or on the newer roads infested with trams, cars and human traffic is dead-easy if you happen to have been the stunt driver in *Ronin*, but not so easy for the rest of us. It's not worth steering your way around this increasingly congested city unless you plan to make lots of trips to outlying suburbs or regional areas; for just about everywhere else, public transport does nicely.

Where it's not restricted to permit-owning residents, parking on the street in Praha 1 involves parking meters that swallow 30-40Kč/hr for a maximum time of 2-6 hours; parking is free on Sunday. There are also several underground car parks charging an average of 40Kč for the first two hours and 30Kč for each successive hour; try the main train station, Kotva

department store, or the Inter-Continental Hotel.

Road Rules

The three golden rules are: drive on the right-hand side of the road, wear a seatbelt, and under no circumstances slow down at a pedestrian crossing (though there's a new law requiring drivers to yield to pedestrians at crossings, it seems to be taking quite a while to sink in).

The speed limit is 50km/h in built-up areas, 90km/h on major roads, and 130km/h on the highway. Don't risk drinking anything and driving as there's a zero blood-alcohol level requirement for motorists. And stay off that mobile unless you have a hands-free kit.

Rental

Mainstream firms with offices out at the airport are Avis (☎ 20 11 42 70; e www.avis.cz; 2300-5100Kč/day; airport pick-up surcharge included in daily rental), Hertz (☎ 20 10 24 24; e www.hertz.cz; 2250-8000Kč/day; airport pick-up surcharge 15% of daily rental) and Europcar (☎ 35 36 45 31; e www.europcar.cz; 1800-8000Kč/day; airport pick-up surcharge 14% of daily rental).

Driving Licence & Permit

Your home-country drivers' licence will do as long as it includes your photo, otherwise you'll need an International Driving Permit.

Motoring Organisations

ÚAMK (Automoto-Klub; ☎ 1230, main office 61 10 43 33) offers 24hr road service to affiliated members of national organisations; the un-affiliated will need to pay for assistance. Autoklub Bohemia Assistance (ABA; ☎ 1240, info 26 14 91) also offers 24hr breakdown service.

PRACTICAL INFORMATION

Climate & When to Go

Tourists come to Prague year-round, but are especially thick on the ground from May to June and over Easter, Christmas and New Year's, when getting across Charles Bridge quickly is impossible without a catapult. May and September, the months on either side of the hot, downpour-prone summer, usually have the best weather for exploring the city on foot. Though the snowy winters get very cold and are susceptible to smog alerts, it can be a beautiful time to visit and accommodation is plentiful. From the beginning of the low season in October, many attractions and businesses start limiting their hours, or go into hibernation until the following summer.

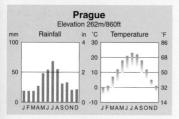

Tourist Information

Tourist Information Abroad

Information on the Czech Republic can be found overseas in the representative offices of the Czech Tourist Authority (ČCCR; **e** www .visitczech.cz). ČCCR offices abroad include:

Canada
  Suite 1510, Simpson Tower, 401 Bay St, Toronto, Ontario M5H2Y4
  (☎ 416-363 99 28)

Germany
  Karl Liebknecht Str 34, 10178 Berlin
  (☎ 30-204 47 70)

UK
  95 Great Portland St, London W1N 5RA
  (☎ 207-291 99 25)

USA
  1109-1111 Madison Ave, New York, NY 10028 (☎ 212-288 08 30)

Local Tourist Information

The city-run Prague Information Service (Pražská informační služba, or PIS; ☎ 124 44; **e** www.prague-info.cz) has four offices offering a wealth of material on the city; pick up the quarterly *Welcome to Prague* plus *Prague This Month*. The branches are located at Old Town Hall (7, C5), Na Příkopě 20 (7, D10), the main train station (3, G12), and Malá Strana Bridge Tower at Mostecká 2 (3, E1; closed Nov-Mar). The Old Town Hall PIS teeters between helpfulness and bored indifference, but it does host a counter belonging to the affiliated Pragotur, which can provide guides.

The private Prague Tourist Centre (Rytířská 12; 7, F6; ☎ 24 23 60 47) sells guidebooks, maps and tickets to concerts and theatre around town.

Embassies & Consulates

Australia
  Unit 6/3, Solitaire Office Building, Klimentská 10, Praha 1
  (3, B10; ☎ 51 01 83 50)

Canada
  Mickiewiczova 6, Praha 6
  (4, D6; ☎ 72 10 18 00)

Germany
  Vlašská 19, Praha 1
  (2, E2; ☎ 57 11 31 11)

New Zealand
  Dykova 19, Praha 1
  (4, F10; ☎ 22 51 46 72)

South Africa
  Ruská 65, Praha 10
  (4, F10; ☎ 67 31 11 14)

UK
  Thunovská 14, Praha 1
  (2, D4; ☎ 57 53 02 78)

USA
  Tržiště 15, Praha 1 (2, E4; ☎ 57 53 06 63)

Money

Currency

The Czech currency is the *koruna* (crown), contracted from *koruna česka* to Kč. Each koruna is divided into 100 *haléřů* or heller (h). Coins come in 10 haléřů , 20 haléřů , 50 haléřů, 1Kč, 2Kč, 5Kč, 10Kč, 20Kč and 50Kč pieces. Notes come in denominations of 20Kč, 50Kč, 100Kč, 200Kč, 500Kč, 1000Kč, 2000Kč and 5000Kč.

Travellers Cheques

Most of the mainstream tourist places will accept travellers cheques from American Express (7, B5; ☎ 24 81 83 88) and Thomas Cook (3, H7; ☎ 21 10 53 71), but smaller businesses may refuse them.

Credit Cards

American Express, Diners Club, Visa and MasterCard/Eurocard are all widely accepted. For 24hr card cancellations or assistance, call:

American Express	☎ 22 80 01 11
Diners Club	☎ 67 31 44 85
Visa	☎ 24 12 53 53
MasterCard/Eurocard	☎ 67 19 74 50

ATMs

There's no shortage of ATMs around Prague, particularly in the areas where plastic-happy people congregate, like Na Příkopě, Wenceslas Square, náměstí Republiky, the main train station and the airport. All ATMS will process cards belonging to or affiliated with Maestro, MasterCard, Visa, Plus and Cirrus.

Changing Money

The best place to change money is at one of the big banks, where commissions usually hover around 0-2%. The worst place to change money is at one of the myriad private bureaux *(směnárna)* around Wenceslas Square and throughout the Old Town. Many of these typically advertise zero commission, which sounds terrific until you find out this percentage applies only to the selling of currency (ie, selling you foreign currency in exchange for your koruna). When you are buying local currency, the commission they charge can be as high as 10%. Avoid 5000Kč and 2000Kč notes, as these can be extremely difficult to change.

Banks are generally open Mon-Fri 8am-5pm, but counters are sometimes temporarily unattended around lunchtime.

Tipping

Some restaurants indicate on their menus or on your itemised bill that the final amount includes a tip; check to make sure you don't tip twice. Where you feel service warrants a gratuity, tip 10-15% extra.

Discounts

Students, children under 15 and families get discounts at most tourist attractions and on public transport (children get a single fare for 50% less). Some performance venues offer reductions, but many just have different levels of fixed-price seating. Seniors need to be Czech citizens to qualify for the relevant local concession card; the same applies to disabled travellers. That said, a number of places will grant concessions regardless of the formalities, and others will only have a cursory glance at the card you're waving at them.

The Prague Card offers three days of unlimited public transport and access to many museums and galleries. It's available from American Express (Staroměstské náměstí; 7, B5), Čedok (Na Příkopě 18; 7, E9), and several other travel agencies, and costs 560/460Kč.

Youth Cards

Bring an international student identity card (ISIC). Youth cards like Euro26 and Go25 will also get you discounts at many museums, theatres and galleries, plus some hotels. HI members often still receive discounts at the hostels in Czech Republic that are not part of the HI network.

Travel Insurance

A policy covering theft, loss, medical expenses and compensation for cancellation or delays in your travel arrangements is highly recommended. If items are lost or stolen, make sure you get a police report straight away (see Safety Concerns, p. 118) – otherwise your insurer might not pay up.

Opening Hours

The following hours are just a rough guide, and can fluctuate wildly according to the type of business, season and location; note that tourist-oriented places are generally open longer hours and often on Sunday.

Shops
    Mon-Fri 9am-6pm, Sat 10am-1pm

Offices
    Mon-Fri 9am-5pm

Restaurants
    11am-11pm

Attractions
    10am-6pm; many museums and galleries closed Mon

Public Holidays

1 Jan	New Year's Day
Mar/Apr	Easter Monday
1 May	Labour Day
8 May	Liberation Day
5 Jul	SS Cyril & Methodius Day
6 Jul	Jan Hus Day
28 Sept	Czech Statehood Day
28 Oct	Independence Day
17 Nov	Struggle for Freedom & Democracy Day
24 Dec	'Generous Day', Christmas Eve
25 Dec	Christmas Day
26 Dec	St Stephen's Day

Time

Czechs use the 24hr clock. Prague Standard Time is 1hr ahead of GMT/UTC. Daylight-savings time is practised from the last weekend in March to the last weekend of October. At noon in Prague it's:

        6am in New York
        3am in Los Angeles
        11am in London
        1pm in Johannesburg
        9pm in Sydney
        11pm in Auckland

Electricity

Electricity in Prague is 220V, 50Hz. Sockets have two round holes; some have a protruding earth (ground) pin. Bring international plug adaptors with you as they're difficult to find locally. Note that North Americans need to bring a transformer to operate their 110V appliances. Laptop users should make sure their batteries are charged, as power cuts are not unknown in mid-range hotels with dubious wiring.

Weights & Measures

The metric system is used. Czechs use commas rather than decimal points, and points for thousands. Prices rounded to the nearest koruna are followed by a dash. See the conversion table (p. 122).

Post

Prague's postal service is fairly reliable, but for important items it's best to use registered mail *(doporučený dopis)* or Express Mail Service (EMS). The main post office (Jindřišská 14; 3, G10; ☎ 21 13 11 11) has an automated queuing system. Dispensers in the entrance hall issue tickets; there are instructions in English on the machines, and an information desk inside the main hall to the left. Stamps can be bought at any newsstand.

Postal Rates

Standard mail to domestic destinations costs 5.40Kč. Postcards/letters to elsewhere in Europe cost 7/9Kč, and to Australia, USA and Canada 10/14Kč.

Opening Hours

Most post offices are open Mon-Fri 8am-6pm or 7pm and Sat to noon. The exceptions are the main post office, which is open 7am-8pm for sending postage and parcels, and the post office located at Hybernská 15 (3, E13), which stays open 12.30am-11.30pm.

Telephone

Prague telephone numbers have been earmarked for some widespread changes in September 2002. If you find that a number listed in this guide doesn't work, call local directory assistance (☎ 1180).

Local calls at peak times (Mon-Fri 7am-7pm) from fixed phones attract charges of 1.30Kč/min, while calls from phone booths cost 3Kč/3min; rates fall by around 50% outside peak times. Note that blue phones only take coins (2-20Kč) but there are plenty of cardphones that use phonecards *(telekart)* suitable for local, domestic and international calls.

Phonecards

A variety of phonecards are available from the PIS, post offices and newsagents in 50-unit (175Kč) and 100-unit (320Kč) versions. Lonely Planet's eKno Communication Card, specifically aimed at travellers, provides competitive international calls (avoid using it for local calls), messaging services and free email. Log on to **e** www.ekno.lonelyplanet.com for information on joining and accessing the service.

Mobile Phones

The mobile phone network is GSM 900, which is compatible with other European and Australian phones but not with Japanese or North American models (though GSM 1800 and PCS 1900 mobiles should work). Check with your local provider as to the status and required set-up of your phone before leaving home. To call a Czech mobile phone from abroad, drop the initial '0' in the 10-digit number.

Country & City Codes

Czech Republic	☎ 420
Prague	☎ 2

Useful Numbers

Local Directory Inquiries	☎ 1180
International Directory Inquiries	☎ 1181
International Operator	☎ 133 004
Reverse-Charge (collect)	☎ 133 004
Time	☎ 14112
Wake-up Calls	☎ 133 000

International Direct Dial Codes

Dial 00 followed by:

Australia	☎ 61
Canada	☎ 1
Japan	☎ 81
New Zealand	☎ 64
South Africa	☎ 27
UK	☎ 44
USA	☎ 1

Email/www

The Internet cafe is a growing phenomenon in Prague – very useful if your accommodation is not connected. However, nearly all top-end hotels have on-site facilities or data points in rooms, while Internet-cafe connection speeds and charges can vary significantly, with the terminal-heavy places usually charging the lowest prices; some also have data points for plugging in your laptop.

Internet Service Providers (ISPs)

Major ISPs you can access in Prague include AOL (dial-in code ☎ 22 10 10 10, [e] www.aol.com), CompuServe (dial-in code ☎ 22 10 10 10, [e] www.compuserve.com) and AT&T (dial-in code ☎ 67 09 01 16, [e] www.attbusiness.net).

Internet Cafes

blue@mail
Konviktská 8 (3, H5; ☎ 24 25 67 25; [e] www.bluemail.cz; Mon-Fri 10am-10pm, Sat-Sun 10am-11pm; 40Kč/30mins, cheaper rates after first hour)

Bohemia Bagel
Újezd 16 (2, H5; ☎ 57 31 06 94; [e] info@bohemiabagel.cz; www.bohemiabagel.cz; Mon-Fri 7am-midnight, Sat-Sun 8am-midnight; 1.50Kč/min)

The Globe
Pštrossova 6 (3, K5; ☎ 24 91 62 64; [e] info@globe.cz; www.globebookstore.cz; 10am-midnight; 1Kč/min)

Internet Café Prague
Karlova 25 (7, D4; ☎ 21 08 52 84; [e] internetcafe@internetcafe.cz; www.internetcafe.cz; 10am-midnight; 30Kč/15min – pricey, but cheaper rates for long-term use)

Useful Sites

The Lonely Planet website (you'll find it at [e] www.lonelyplanet.com) offers a speedy link to many of Prague's best websites. Others to try include:

Radio Free Europe/Radio Liberty
[e] www.rferl.org/bd/cz

Prague Business Journal
[e] www.pbj.cz/user/index.asp

Prague Contact
[e] www.praguecontact.com

Prague Castle
[e] www.hrad.cz

Theatre Institute Prague
[e] www.theatre.cz

Doing Business

The business centre at the Renaissance Prague Hotel (V Celnici 7; 3, D11; ☎ 21 82 11 11; [e] www.renaissancehotels.com) has workstations for rent as well as Internet access. Other services available include typing, printing from disk, photocopying and faxing. If you need translation work done, try the reputable Artlingua (Myslíkova 6; 4, F7; ☎ 24 91 80 58; [e] www.artlingua.cz) or the Czech Association of Conference Interpreters (Přemyslovská 34; 4, F10; ☎ 22 71 41 20; [e] www.askot.cz).

The trade section of your embassy in Prague should be able to help you get started on business matters. The American Chamber of Commerce (Malá Štupartská 7; 7, B8; AmCham; ☎ 24 82 65 51; [e] www.amcham.cz) is a good resource and produce a number of helpful business reference publications. You'll find that another useful contact is the Economic Chamber of the Czech Republic (Seifertova 22; 4, E9; ☎ 24 09 61 11; e www.hkcr.cz).

Newspapers & Magazines

The main Czech-language daily newspapers include *Mladá fronta Dnes* and the conservative *Lidové noviny*, while the prime English-language newspaper is the rather informal, review-packed weekly *The Prague Post*. The free monthly English/Czech magazine *Think* is a catalogue of trendiness masquerading as deep thought. Major newspapers and magazines from around the world are available at the newsstands populating the tourist areas.

Radio

Local FM radio stations specialise in country (Country Radio; 89.5), classical (Classic; 98.7), disco (Zlatá Praha; 97.2), pop (Bonton; 99.7), and hip alternative music for the masses (Radio 1; 91.9). The state-owned broadcaster is Czech Radio; its news bulletins are available daily at the Radio Prague website (e www.radio.cz).

For English-language news and culture, simply switch over to the BBC World Service (101.1), which re-broadcasts in Czech, Slovak and English. There's also Radio Free Europe (1233, 1287AM), which operates out of the building next to the National Museum.

TV

There are two government-run television channels, ČT1 and ČT2, the latter broadcasting the English-language 'Euronews' at either noon or 1pm. There are also two private channels – Nova and Prima – that fail to graduate from trashy sitcoms and soaps. Most hotels and rented apartments have satellite receivers, allegedly broadening your small-screen choices.

Photography & Video

Film-processing places are in abundant supply, particularly in the Old Town and Malá Strana; there are a couple of decent shops in the Kotva (7, A10) and Krone (3, H9) department stores. You can entrust your slides to Fotografia Praha (3, J8) or to Fototechnika (3, H9); both use a reliable lab and are located in Lucerna Passage. Fototechnika is also a dependable place for camera repairs.

The Czech Republic uses the PAL video system, which is incompatible with the SECAM (France) or NTSC (Japan and North America) systems. Make sure you double-check which system your own equipment is based on.

Health

Immunisations
It's not necessary to get any vaccinations prior to your trip to the Czech Republic, unless there's a shot you can get that makes you completely impervious to bad airline movies.

Precautions
Prague enjoys a good standard of public hygiene, both in its restaurants and in its utilities, though you may not think so if you taste the unpleasantly chlorinated but nonetheless drinkable tap water. A less innocuous health risk is posed by the exhaust emissions that can cloud the city in winter during periods of extremely stable

weather (known in meteorological terms as inversions).

Like anywhere else, practise the usual precautions when it comes to sex; condoms are available at any of the many pharmacies (*lekárna*). See the following Pharmacies section for some 24hr places.

Insurance & Medical Treatment

Travel insurance is advisable to cover medical treatment you may need while in Prague. First-aid outside a hospital (*nemocnice*) and emergency treatment are provided free to visitors, but unless you are a EU citizen covered under a reciprocal health-care arrangement, you will have to pay full price for treatment. The cost of prescriptions is borne by all foreigners.

Medical Services

Hospitals and clinics with 24hr emergency departments include:

Na Homolce
  Roentgenova 2, Motol, Praha 5 (4, F1; ☎ 57 27 21 46, after hours 57 27 25 27)

Policlinic at Národní
  Národní 9, Staré Město, Praha 1 (3, H5; ☎ 22 07 51 20, after hours 0606-461 628, children's clinic 24 94 77 17)

Health Centre Prague
  No 3, 2nd fl, Vodičkova 28, Nové Město, Praha 1 (3, J8; ☎ 24 22 00 40, after hours 0603-433 833)

Dental Services

For emergency treatment, head to the 24hr Praha 1 clinic (Palackého 5, Nové Město; 3, H8; ☎ 24 94 69 81).

Pharmacies

The following pharmacies are open 24 hours:

Lékárna Palackého
  Praha 1 clinic, Palackého 5, Nové Město, Praha 1 (3, H8; ☎ 24 94 69 81)

Lékárna U sv Ludmily
  Belgická 37, Vinohrady, Praha 2 (6 D2; ☎ 22 51 33 96)

Lékárna U Anděla
  Štefánikova 6, Praha 5 (4, F6; ☎ 57 32 09 18)

Toilets

Public toilets (*vé cé* or *toalet*) for men (marked *muži* or *páni*) and women (marked *ženy* or *dámy*) located in metro, train and bus stations will normally be staffed by attendants whose wages are paid by the 2-3Kč you give them for use of the facilities. Toilets in tourist attractions such as museums can be used free of charge.

Safety Concerns

Pickpocketing is a problem in places where tourists congregate, like Charles Bridge, Wenceslas Square and the main train station. It can also affect crowds waiting for either the Astronomical Clock or the guards outside Prague Castle to do their thang. Visitors have also been targeted by men posing as police – one version of this scam involves the 'cops' asking to see the foreigner's money and then returning it minus a few notes. If you doubt the authenticity of an official who approaches you, hang on to your wallet and passport and insist on going with them to the nearest police station. To make a police report regarding stolen property, head to the interpreter-equipped Praha 1 police station at Jungmannovo náměstí 9 (3, G8; ☎ 61 45 17 60).

Prague is a safe city to walk around at night if you apply the usual common sense and stay aware of your surroundings. At night, avoid the park in front of the main train station.

Lost Property

Try the city's lost and found office (Karoliny Světlé 5; 3, H5; ztráty a nálezy; ☎ 24 23 50 85; open Mon & Wed 8am-noon & 12.30-5.30pm, Tues & Thurs 8am-noon & 12.30-4pm, Fri 8am-noon & 12.30-2pm). Ruzyně airport has a 24hr lost and found office (☎ 20 11 42 83).

Keeping Copies

Make photocopies of all your important documents, keep some with you, separate from the originals, and leave a copy at home. You can also store details of documents in Lonely Planet's free online Travel Vault, password-protected and accessible worldwide. See e www .ekno.lonelyplanet.com.

Emergency Numbers

Ambulance	☎ 155
Fire	☎ 150
Police (municipal)	☎ 156
Police (national)	☎ 158
Rape Crisis Line	☎ 57 31 71 00
(Mon-Fri 9am-5pm)	

Women Travellers

Prague is a safe city for women in direct comparison to other large European cities, but there has been a rise in the incidence of sexual violence towards women over the past decade, and verbal harassment is not uncommon.

Women, particularly those travelling solo, may find many neighbourhood pubs (the ones frequented by locals rather than tourists) less enjoyable because of their complete domination by the Y chromosome. If that's the case, don't fret – there are still plenty of relaxed *vinárny* (wine bars) and alcohol-serving *kavárny* (coffee shops) to discover.

For tampons and pads, go to the nearest *lékárna* or department store supermarkets like the one in the basement of Tesco (3, H6). To get the contraceptive pill, you need a prescription.

Gay & Lesbian Travellers

Homosexuality is legal in Czech Republic and the age of consent is 15. The gay scene in Prague is thriving, with a fair number of clubs, bars, restaurants and hotels catering to the community. It's a discreet scene, however, with the various venues scattered across different areas and little in the way of mainstream events to draw attention to gay life. Several establishments tailor themselves to both gays and lesbians, but the majority are gay-oriented; only one place (A-Club; see p. 98) reserves evenings for lesbians. Visiting gay couples may trigger uncomfortable reactions from some locals if they display affection in public, as it remains an unfamiliar sight to many Czechs.

Information & Organisations

Extensive information on gay and lesbian happenings and resources is presented online by GayGuide.net Prague (e www.gayguide.net/ Europe/Czech/Prague). *Amigo* is a bi-monthly gay publication with venue/event information and lots of classifieds, while two irregularly published Czech-language lesbian magazines are *Promluv* and *Alia*.

Senior Travellers

Some senior visitors may find the constant skipping over the often loose cobblestones of the Old Town a bit of a chore, and the same might be said of jumping on and off narrow sidewalks to avoid collisions with oncoming groups. Allow plenty of time for exploring your chosen neighbourhood. Another potential frustration is accommodation with several floors but no elevator – ask questions about the facilities when making a booking.

Disabled Travellers

Prague is making an effort to address the needs of disabled travellers, though facilities in some areas are still sorely lacking. Wheelchair-accessible public transport is limited to several train and metro stations with self-operating lifts, plus special buses plying two routes on weekdays linking destinations such as Hradčanská, Florenc and Náměstí Republiky; there are also two dozen mainly suburban lines serviced by low-platform buses. Pedestrian-crossing lights in the centre make a ticking noise to indicate a green light to the visually impaired, and some museums now have tactile displays and Braille text. More performance venues are being equipped with wheelchair access and some have good facilities for the hearing impaired.

Information & Organisations

A comprehensive source of information for wheelchair-bound travellers is the Prague Wheelchair Users Organisation (Benediktská 6, Josefov; 3, C9; Pražská organizace vozíčkářů; ☎ 24 82 72 10, e www .pov.cz). It produces the booklet Barrier-Free Prague, listing accessible venues, reserved parking places, transport options and tours of historical areas. The Czech-language monthly Přehled also lists wheelchair-friendly venues.

The Union of the Blind and Weak Sighted (Krakovská 21; 3, K10; Sjednocená organizace nevidomých a slabozrakých v Čr; ☎ 96 23 11 08) can provide information to the vision-impaired.

Language

Czech (čeština) is obviously the main language spoken in the Czech Republic. English is widespread in central Prague but not commonly spoken in the outer suburbs and the countryside – 'widespread' doesn't mean 'always', however, and you'll often encounter people in the tourist industry who speak very little or no English. Many older citizens also speak German.

Originating from a west Slavonic linguistic grouping, Czech can prove to be a mouthful for first-time speakers, particularly the words that are vowel-free zones. However, it doesn't take that long to begin wrapping your tongue around some of the more commonly uttered words and phrases, and the effort is often appreciated by locals. For a more detailed look at the language, get a copy of Lonely Planet's Central Europe phrasebook or Eastern Europe phrasebook.

Useful Words & Phrases

Good day.	Dobrý den.
Goodbye.	Na shledanou.
Hello/Goodbye.	Ahoj/Čau. (ciao) (informal)
How are you?	Jak se máte?
Fine, thanks.	Děkuji, dobře.
Yes.	Ano/Jo.
No.	Ne.
Excuse me.	S dovolením.
Sorry. (excuse me, forgive me)	Promiňte.
Please.	Prosím.
Thank you (very much).	(Mockrát) děkuji.
That's fine/ You're welcome.	Není zač.
Do you speak English?	Mluvíte anglicky?
I don't understand.	Nerozumím.

Getting Around

What time does ... leave/ arrive?	*V kolik hodin odjíždí/ přijíždí ...?*
the train	*vlak*
the bus	*autobus*

Which platform?	*Které nástupiště?*
Excuse me, where is ...?	*Prosím, kde je ...?*
I'm looking for ...	*Hledám ...*
(the) ticket office	*pokladna*
I want to go to ...	*Chci jet do ...*
Go straight ahead.	*Jděte přímo.*
Turn left.	*Zatočte vlevo.*
Turn right.	*Zatočte vpravo.*

Buying Tickets

I'd like ...	*Rád (m) bych ...*
	Ráda (f) bych ...
a one-way ticket	*jednosměrnou jízdenku*
a return ticket	*zpáteční jízdenku*
two tickets	*dvě jízdenky*

Accommodation

Do you have any rooms available?	*Máte volné pokoje?*
I'd like ...	*Přál (m) bych si ...*
	Přála (f) bych si ...
a single room	*jednolůžkový pokoj*
a double room	*dvoulůžkový pokoj*
How much is it per night?	*Kolik stojí jedna noc?*

Around Town

bank	*banka*
embassy	*velvyslanectví*
information centre	*informační centrum*
main square	*hlavní náměstí*
market	*tržiště/trh*
theatre	*divadlo*
train station	*ČD/železniční nádraží*

Time & Dates

What time is it?	*Kolik je hodin?*
When?	*Kdy?*

in the morning	*ráno*
in the afternoon	*odpoledne*
in the evening	*večer*
today	*dnes*
now	*teď*

Monday	*pondělí*
Tuesday	*úterý*
Wednesday	*středa*
Thursday	*čtvrtek*
Friday	*pátek*
Saturday	*sobota*
Sunday	*neděle*

January	*leden*
February	*únor*
March	*březen*
April	*duben*
May	*květen*
June	*červen*
July	*červenec*
August	*srpen*
September	*září*
October	*říjen*
November	*listopad*
December	*prosinec*

Numbers

0	*nula*	7	*sedm*
1	*jeden*	8	*osm*
2	*dva*	9	*devět*
3	*tři*	10	*deset*
4	*čtyři*	50	*padesát*
5	*pět*	100	*sto*
6	*šest*	1000	*tisíc*

Emergencies

Help!	*Pomoc!*
I'm ill.	*Jsem nemocný/ nemocná. (m/f)*
Please call a doctor.	*Prosím, zavolejte doktora.*
ambulance	*sanitku*
police	*policii*
Where is the toilet?	*Kde je záchod?*
I'm lost.	*Zabloudil /a jsem. (m/f)*
Could you help me please?	*Prosím, můžete mi pomoci?*

Conversion Table

Clothing Sizes
Measurements approximate only; try before you buy.

Women's Clothing

Aust/NZ	8	10	12	14	16	18
Europe	36	38	40	42	44	46
Japan	5	7	9	11	13	15
UK	8	10	12	14	16	18
USA	6	8	10	12	14	16

Women's Shoes

Aust/NZ	5	6	7	8	9	10
Europe	35	36	37	38	39	40
France only	35	36	38	39	40	42
Japan	22	23	24	25	26	27
UK	3½	4½	5½	6½	7½	8½
USA	5	6	7	8	9	10

Men's Clothing

Aust/NZ	92	96	100	104	108	112
Europe	46	48	50	52	54	56
Japan	S		M	M		L
UK	35	36	37	38	39	40
USA	35	36	37	38	39	40

Men's Shirts (Collar Sizes)

Aust/NZ	38	39	40	41	42	43
Europe	38	39	40	41	42	43
Japan	38	39	40	41	42	43
UK	15	15½	16	16½	17	17½
USA	15	15½	16	16½	17	17½

Men's Shoes

Aust/NZ	7	8	9	10	11	12
Europe	41	42	43	44½	46	47
Japan	26	27	27.5	28	29	30
UK	7	8	9	10	11	12
USA	7½	8½	9½	10½	11½	12½

Weights & Measures

Weight

1kg = 2.2lb
1lb = 0.45kg
1g = 0.04oz
1oz = 28g

Volume

1 litre = 0.26 US gallons
1 US gallon = 3.8 litres
1 litre = 0.22 imperial gallons
1 imperial gallon = 4.55 litres

Length & Distance

1 inch = 2.54cm
1cm = 0.39 inches
1m = 3.3ft = 1.1yds
1ft = 0.3m
1km = 0.62 miles
1 mile = 1.6km

lonely planet

Lonely Planet is the world's most successful independent travel information company with offices in Australia, the US, UK and France. With a reputation for comprehensive, reliable travel information, Lonely Planet is a print and electronic publishing leader, with over 650 titles and 22 series catering for travellers' individual needs.

At Lonely Planet we believe that travellers can make a positive contribution to the countries they visit – if they respect their host communities and spend their money wisely. Since 1986 a percentage of the income from books has been donated to aid and human rights projects.

www.lonelyplanet.com

For news, views and free subscriptions to print and email newsletters, and a full list of LP titles, click on Lonely Planet's award-winning website.

On the Town

A romantic escape to Paris or a mad shopping dash through New York City, the locals' secret bars or a city's top attractions – whether you have 24 hours to kill or months to explore, Lonely Planet's On the Town products will give you the low-down.

Condensed guides are ideal pocket guides for when time is tight. Their quick-view maps, full-colour layout and opinionated reviews help short-term visitors target the top sights and discover the very best eating, shopping and entertainment options a city has to offer.

For more indepth coverage, **City guides** offer insights into a city's character and cultural background as well as providing broad coverage of where to eat, stay and play. **CitySync**, a digital guide for your handheld unit, allows you to reference stacks of opinionated, well-researched travel information. Portable and durable **City Maps** are perfect for locating those back-street bars or hard-to-find local haunts.

'Ideal for a generation of fast movers.'

– *Gourmet Traveller* on Condensed guides

Condensed Guides

- Amsterdam
- Athens
- Bangkok (Sept 2002)
- Barcelona
- Boston
- Chicago
- Dublin
- Frankfurt
- Hong Kong
- London
- Los Angeles (Oct 2002)
- New York City
- Paris
- Prague
- Rome
- San Francisco (Oct 2002)
- Singapore (Oct 2002)
- Sydney
- Tokyo
- Venice
- Washington DC

index

See also separate indexes for Places to Eat (p. 126), Places to Stay (p. 127), Shops (p. 127) and Sights with map references (p. 128).

PLACES TO EAT

PLACES TO STAY

SHOPS

sights – quick index